Adam Smith and the Economy of the Passions

The fertility of Adam Smith's work stems from a paradoxical structure where the pursuit of economic self-interest and wealth accumulation serve wider social objectives. The incentive for this wealth accumulation comes from a desire for social recognition or 'sympathy' – the need to recognise ourselves in our peers – which is the primary incentive for moderating and transforming our violent and egotistical passions. Adam Smith thus examines in detail the subliminal emotional structure underlying market behaviour.

This new book by Professor Jan Horst Keppler presents an Adam Smith for the twenty-first century, more sceptical, searching and daring than he has ever been portrayed before. Without disputing its benefits, Professor Keppler's original contribution explores the anarchic passions constantly threatening to destroy all social bounds, and how the overarching 'desire for love' and social recognition provides the Smithian individual with the incentive to transform his unsocial passions into a desire for social advancement and economic wealth with the view to gaining the vital approbation of his peers. One of the most striking results of this new reading of Adam Smith is the latter's insistence on the primacy of exchange value over use value. In other words, the quest for wealth is exclusively driven by the value it represents in the eyes of others rather than by any value in individual use.

At a moment of crisis, where the link between 'true' economic values and 'virtual' financial values is more fragile than ever, Adam Smith's work is a profoundly contemporary reminder that in the absence of personal, ethical groundings our economic actions are only grounded in the game of mirrors we play with our peers. This book will be of interest to postgraduate students and researchers in the History of Economics, or indeed any reader with an interest in the psychological foundations of a market economy and its theoretical representations as developed by Adam Smith.

Jan Horst Keppler is Professor of Economics at the University Paris – Dauphine and Senior Researcher at PHARE Institute on the History and Epistemology of Economics at the University Paris I Pantheon – Sorbonne.

Routledge studies in the history of economics

1. **Economics as Literature**
   Willie Henderson

2. **Socialism and Marginalism in Economics 1870–1930**
   Edited by Ian Steedman

3. **Hayek's Political Economy**
   The socio-economics of order
   Steve Fleetwood

4. **On the Origins of Classical Economics**
   Distribution and value from William Petty to Adam Smith
   Tony Aspromourgos

5. **The Economics of Joan Robinson**
   Edited by Maria Cristina Marcuzzo, Luigi Pasinetti and Alesandro Roncaglia

6. **The Evolutionist Economics of Léon Walras**
   Albert Jolink

7. **Keynes and the 'Classics'**
   A study in language, epistemology and mistaken identities
   Michel Verdon

8. **The History of Game Theory, Vol 1**
   From the beginnings to 1945
   Robert W. Dimand and Mary Ann Dimand

9. **The Economics of W. S. Jevons**
   Sandra Peart

10. **Gandhi's Economic Thought**
Ajit K. Dasgupta

11. **Equilibrium and Economic Theory**
Edited by Giovanni Caravale

12. **Austrian Economics in Debate**
Edited by Willem Keizer, Bert Tieben and Rudy van Zijp

13. **Ancient Economic Thought**
Edited by B.B. Price

14. **The Political Economy of Social Credit and Guild Socialism**
Frances Hutchinson and Brian Burkitt

15. **Economic Careers**
Economics and economists in Britain 1930–70
Keith Tribe

16. **Understanding 'Classical' Economics**
Studies in the long-period theory
Heinz Kurz and Neri Salvadori

17. **History of Environmental Economic Thought**
E. Kula

18. **Economic Thought in Communist and Post-Communist Europe**
Edited by Hans-Jürgen Wagener

19. **Studies in the History of French Political Economy**
From Bodin to Walras
Edited by Gilbert Faccarello

20. **The Economics of John Rae**
Edited by O.F. Hamouda, C. Lee and D. Mair

21. **Keynes and the Neoclassical Synthesis**
Einsteinian versus Newtonian macroeconomics
Teodoro Dario Togati

22. **Historical Perspectives on Macroeconomics**
Sixty years after the 'General Theory'
Edited by Philippe Fontaine and Albert Jolink

23. **The Founding of Institutional Economics**
    The leisure class and sovereignty
    Edited by Warren J. Samuels

24. **Evolution of Austrian Economics**
    From Menger to Lachmann
    Sandye Gloria

25. **Marx's Concept of Money**
    The God of commodities
    Anitra Nelson

26. **The Economics of James Steuart**
    Edited by Ramón Tortajada

27. **The Development of Economics in Europe since 1945**
    Edited by A.W. Bob Coats

28. **The Canon in the History of Economics**
    Critical essays
    Edited by Michalis Psalidopoulos

29. **Money and Growth**
    Selected papers of Allyn Abbott Young
    Edited by Perry G. Mehrling and Roger J. Sandilands

30. **The Social Economics of Jean-Baptiste Say**
    Markets and virtue
    Evelyn L. Forget

31. **The Foundations of Laissez-Faire**
    The economics of Pierre de Boisguilbert
    Gilbert Faccarello

32. **John Ruskin's Political Economy**
    Willie Henderson

33. **Contributions to the History of Economic Thought**
    Essays in honour of R.D.C. Black
    Edited by Antoin E. Murphy and Renee Prendergast

34. **Towards an Unknown Marx**
A commentary on the manuscripts of 1861–63
Enrique Dussel

35. **Economics and Interdisciplinary Exchange**
Edited by Guido Erreygers

36. **Economics as the Art of Thought**
Essays in memory of G.L.S. Shackle
Edited by Stephen F. Frowen and Peter Earl

37. **The Decline of Ricardian Economics**
Politics and economics in post-Ricardian theory
Susan Pashkoff

38. **Piero Sraffa**
His life, thought and cultural heritage
Alessandro Roncaglia

39. **Equilibrium and Disequilibrium in Economic Theory**
The Marshall–Walras divide
Michel de Vroey

40. **The German Historical School**
The historical and ethical approach to economics
Edited by Yuichi Shionoya

41. **Reflections on the Classical Canon in Economics**
Essays in honour of Samuel Hollander
Edited by Sandra Peart and Evelyn Forget

42. **Piero Sraffa's Political Economy**
A centenary estimate
Edited by Terenzio Cozzi and Roberto Marchionatti

43. **The Contribution of Joseph Schumpeter to Economics**
Economic development and institutional change
Richard Arena and Cecile Dangel

44. **On the Development of Long-run Neo-Classical Theory**
Tom Kompas

45. **F. A. Hayek as a Political Economist**
Economic analysis and values
Edited by Jack Birner, Pierre Garrouste and Thierry Aimar

46. **Pareto, Economics and Society**
The mechanical analogy
Michael McLure

47. **The Cambridge Controversies in Capital Theory**
A study in the logic of theory development
Jack Birner

48. **Economics Broadly Considered**
Essays in honour of Warren J. Samuels
Edited by Steven G. Medema, Jeff Biddle and John B. Davis

49. **Physicians and Political Economy**
Six studies of the work of doctor-economists
Edited by Peter Groenewegen

50. **The Spread of Political Economy and the Professionalisation of Economists**
Economic societies in Europe, America and Japan in the nineteenth century
Massimo Augello and Marco Guidi

51. **Historians of Economics and Economic Thought**
The construction of disciplinary memory
Steven G. Medema and Warren J. Samuels

52. **Competing Economic Theories**
Essays in memory of Giovanni Caravale
Sergio Nisticò and Domenico Tosato

53. **Economic Thought and Policy in Less Developed Europe**
The nineteenth century
Edited by Michalis Psalidopoulos and Maria-Eugenia Almedia Mata

54. **Family Fictions and Family Facts**
Harriet Martineau, Adolphe Quetelet and the population question in England 1798–1859
Brian Cooper

55. **Eighteenth-Century Economics**
Peter Groenewegen

56. **The Rise of Political Economy in the Scottish Enlightenment**
Edited by Tatsuya Sakamoto and Hideo Tanaka

57. **Classics and Moderns in Economics, Volume I**
Essays on nineteenth and twentieth century economic thought
Peter Groenewegen

58. **Classics and Moderns in Economics, Volume II**
Essays on nineteenth and twentieth century economic thought
Peter Groenewegen

59. **Marshall's Evolutionary Economics**
Tiziano Raffaelli

60. **Money, Time and Rationality in Max Weber**
Austrian connections
Stephen D. Parsons

61. **Classical Macroeconomics**
Some modern variations and distortions
James C.W. Ahiakpor

62. **The Historical School of Economics in England and Japan**
Tamotsu Nishizawa

63. **Classical Economics and Modern Theory**
Studies in long-period analysis
Heinz D. Kurz and Neri Salvadori

64. **A Bibliography of Female Economic Thought to 1940**
Kirsten K. Madden, Janet A. Sietz and Michele Pujol

65. **Economics, Economists and Expectations**
From microfoundations to macroeconomics
Warren Young, Robert Leeson and William Darity Jr.

66. **The Political Economy of Public Finance in Britain, 1767–1873**
Takuo Dome

67. **Essays in the History of Economics**
Warren J. Samuels, Willie Henderson, Kirk D. Johnson and Marianne Johnson

68. **History and Political Economy**
Essays in honour of P.D. Groenewegen
Edited by Tony Aspromourgos and John Lodewijks

69. **The Tradition of Free Trade**
Lars Magnusson

70. **Evolution of the Market Process**
Austrian and Swedish economics
Edited by Michel Bellet, Sandye Gloria-Palermo and Abdallah Zouache

71. **Consumption as an Investment**
The fear of goods from Hesiod to Adam Smith
Cosimo Perrotta

72. **Jean-Baptiste Say and the Classical Canon in Economics**
The British connection in French classicism
Samuel Hollander

73. **Knut Wicksell on Poverty**
No place is too exalted
Knut Wicksell

74. **Economists in Cambridge**
A study through their correspondence 1907–46
Edited by M.C. Marcuzzo and A. Rosselli

75. **The Experiment in the History of Economics**
Edited by Philippe Fontaine and Robert Leonard

76. **At the Origins of Mathematical Economics**
The Economics of A.N. Isnard (1748–1803)
Richard van den Berg

77. **Money and Exchange**
Folktales and reality
Sasan Fayazmanesh

78. **Economic Development and Social Change**
Historical roots and modern perspectives
George Stathakis and Gianni Vaggi

79. **Ethical Codes and Income Distribution**
A study of John Bates Clark and Thorstein Veblen
Guglielmo Forges Davanzati

80. **Evaluating Adam Smith**
Creating the wealth of nations
Willie Henderson

81. **Civil Happiness**
Economics and human flourishing in historical perspective
Luigino Bruni

82. **New Voices on Adam Smith**
Edited by Leonidas Montes and Eric Schliesser

83. **Making Chicago Price Theory**
Milton Friedman–George Stigler correspondence, 1945–57
Edited by J. Daniel Hammond and Claire H. Hammond

84. **William Stanley Jevons and the Cutting Edge of Economics**
Bert Mosselmans

85. **A History of Econometrics in France**
From nature to models
Philippe Le Gall

86. **Money and Markets**
A doctrinal approach
Edited by Alberto Giacomin and Maria Cristina Marcuzzo

87. **Considerations on the Fundamental Principles of Pure Political Economy**
Vilfredo Pareto
(Edited by Roberto Marchionatti and Fiorenzo Mornati)

88. **The Years of High Econometrics**
A short history of the generation that reinvented economics
Francisco Louçã

89. **David Hume's Political Economy**
Edited by Carl Wennerlind and Margaret Schabas

90. **Interpreting Classical Economics**
Studies in long-period analysis
Heinz D. Kurz and Neri Salvadori

91. **Keynes's Vision**
Why the great depression did not return
John Philip Jones

92. **Monetary Theory in Retrospect**
The selected essays of Filippo Cesarano
Filippo Cesarano

93. **Keynes's Theoretical Development**
From the tract to the general theory
Toshiaki Hirai

94. **Leading Contemporary Economists**
Economics at the cutting edge
Edited by Steven Pressman

95. **The Science of Wealth**
Adam Smith and the framing of political economy
Tony Aspromourgos

96. **Capital, Time and Transitional Dynamics**
Edited by Harald Hagemann and Roberto Scazzieri

97. **New Essays on Pareto's Economic Theory**
Edited by Luigino Bruni and Aldo Montesano

98. **Frank Knight and the Chicago School in American Economics**
Ross B. Emmett

99. **A History of Economic Theory**
Essays in honour of Takashi Negishi
Edited by Aiko Ikeo and Heinz D. Kurz

100. **Open Economics**
Economics in relation to other disciplines
Edited by Richard Arena, Sheila Dow and Matthias Klaes

101. Rosa Luxemburg and the Critique of Political Economy
Edited by Riccardo Bellofiore

102. Problems and Methods of Econometrics
The Poincaré Lectures of Ragnar Frisch 1933
Edited by Olav Bjerkholt and Ariane Dupont-Keiffer

103. Criticisms of Classical Political Economy
Menger, Austrian economics and the German historical school
Gilles Campagnolo

104. A History of Entrepreneurship
Robert F. Hébert and Albert N. Link

105. Keynes on Monetary Policy, Finance and Uncertainty
Liquidity preference theory and the global financial crisis
Jorg Bibow

106. Kalecki's Principle of Increasing Risk and Keynesian Economics
Tracy Mott

107. Economic Theory and Economic Thought
Essays in honour of Ian Steedman
John Vint, J. Stanley Metcalfe, Heinz D. Kurz, Neri Salvadori and Paul Samuelson

108. Political Economy, Public Policy and Monetary Economics
Ludwig von Mises and the Austrian tradition
Richard M. Ebeling

109. Keynes and the British Humanist Tradition
The moral purpose of the market
David R. Andrews

110. Political Economy and Industrialism
Banks in Saint-Simonian economic thought
Gilles Jacoud

111. Studies in Social Economics
By Leon Walras
Translated by Jan van Daal and Donald Walker

112. The Making of the Classical Theory of Economic Growth
Anthony Brewer

113. The Origins of David Hume's Economics
Willie Henderson

114. Production, Distribution and Trade
Edited by Adriano Birolo, Duncan Foley, Heinz D. Kurz, Bertram Schefold and Ian Steedman

115. The Essential Writings of Thorstein Veblen
Edited by Charles Camic and Geoffrey Hodgson

116. Adam Smith and the Economy of the Passions
Jan Horst Keppler

Adam Smith and the Economy of the Passions

Jan Horst Keppler

Lieber Marc,

Voilà mein Versuch die unsichtbare Hand an der Kreuzung zwischen Ethik und Markt, Gebrauchswert und Tauschwert, Metapher und Metonomie, etwas genauer zu verorten. Beim nächsten Besuch kannst Du mir sagen, was Du davon hältst. Jan

Routledge
Taylor & Francis Group
LONDON AND NEW YORK

First published 2010 by Routledge
2 Park Square, Milton Park, Abingdon, Oxon, OX14 4RN

Simultaneously published in the USA and Canada
by Routledge
270 Madison Avenue, New York, NY 10016

Routledge is an imprint of the Taylor & Francis Group, an informa business

The English version was established by the author on the basis of the French original, *L'Economie des passions selon Adam Smith: les noms du père d'Adam* (Editions Kinè, Paris), and reviewed by Robert Chase, translator

Typeset in Times New Roman by Taylor & Francis Books
Printed and bound in Great Britain by CPI Antony Rowe, Chippenham

British Library Cataloguing in Publication Data
A catalogue record for this book is available from the British Library

Library of Congress Cataloging in Publication Data
Keppler, Jan Horst
[Économie des passions selon Adam Smith. English]
Adam Smith and the economy of the passions / by Jan Horst Keppler; edited by Robert Chase.
p. cm.
Includes bibliographical references and index.
1. Smith, Adam, 1723–1790. 2. Economics–Sociological aspects.
I. Chase, Robert. II. Title.
HB103.S6K4813 2010
330.15'3–dc22 2010001793

ISBN: 978-0-415-56986-6 (hbk)
ISBN: 978-0-203-84756-5 (ebk)

In memory of my father

Contents

In ease of body and peace of mind, all the different ranks of life are nearly upon a level, and the beggar, who suns himself by the side of the highway, possesses that security which kings are fighting for.

Adam Smith, *The Theory of Moral Sentiments*, IV.1.10

1 Introduction

Personal ethics and social morality

1.1 Reading Adam Smith

Do you know Adam Smith, the man, the myth, his work? Certainly somewhat, rather well perhaps. So the answer is 'yes'. Adam Smith remains one of the most influential, the most commented on and even – and this is far from obvious – one of the most read authors in the history of economic thought and even the general history of ideas. Unfortunately, however, this effort often results in the citation of some well-known phrases, which, read out of context, provide more questions than answers.

Readers seeking to go beyond the fixed ideas, the standard opinions and the stock quotations will easily be disoriented by the complexities of a protean work characterised by strong internal tensions and an overabundant secondary literature, unified only by its desire to smooth and simplify this work. For want of being understood, Adam Smith fascinates, but the majority of commentators never feel the need to look into the sources of this fascination. This is unfortunate. The *Adam Smith Problem*, the allusion of a number of diligent nineteenth century academics to a major faultline in Smith's work, is no longer fashionable.

Today, the vast majority of commentators on Adam Smith's major works, *The Theory of Moral Sentiments* and *The Wealth of Nations*, seek to attribute to them *one* sense, *one* well-specified linear interpretation. Most of these contributions are diligent, well-informed and well-intentioned explorations of particular aspects of the work. They may consist of a careful historical or philosophical contextualisation, the recognition of an earlier source of a particular concept, or a classification of modern economic concepts contained, explicitly or implicitly, in Smith's work. Such partial investigations sometimes lead to surprising results. Liberal and anti-liberal economists thus both find support for their positions in a dense and complex work. Neither group, of course, bothers much to search for a fuller truth in the texts beyond the confirmation of conventional positions, most of them well-known in advance.

However, one does not approach a work that has maintained its fascination for more than 200 years, with the intention of silencing it forever. On the contrary, it is necessary to understand the undiminished fertility of the tensions and the wide-ranging implications of the tenuous synthesis that characterise Adam Smith's work. Each generation of scholars and policymakers needs to face these tensions and formulate the resulting synthesis anew to make it pertinent for their time. After all, with Adam Smith we stand both at the dawn of a new scientific discipline and at the beginning of the social organisation which is ours today. For a fuller understanding of Adam Smith, there is only one way: to trust the texts, in particular those of *The Theory of Moral Sentiments* and *The Wealth of Nations*. One needs to approach them with respect, certainly, but with eyes and ears open and with the least amount of prejudice possible.

Very few critics – one may think of David D. Raphael, Vivien Brown or even Jacob Viner – have had the courage to approach Adam Smith's work with a mind sufficiently open to appreciate its heterogeneous elements and its contradictions, all of which contribute to the same radical project. That project is, of course, structured by the convergence of the individual and the general interest, of conscious human intentions and a universal plan of perhaps divine nature. The key issue is that most critics take this convergence as a given, as a hypothesis formulated a priori. They are thus satisfied by commenting on its implications, frequently from an entirely personal perspective. There are not many who have dared, with Adam Smith, to explore the origins of this very particular self-interest, which are hidden in a complex economy of the passions but perfectly elaborated in all their details.

Reading Adam Smith's major works can reserve many a surprise for the amateur as well as for the professional of the history of thought: the apparent lack of any systematic organisation and its tight coherence, its restless and heterogeneous nature, the vast, eclectic and capricious erudition of its author, its pragmatism and its syncretism, its occasional aloofness and its passionate commitment, its literary gems and its set-piece formulas, its humour and its ruthless dedication to a contradictory project and its successful conclusion.

Additional pleasure is provided by Adam Smith's English, which is elaborated with great care. This results from the great prudence with which Smith advances and the underlying tension that characterises his argument. This tension also shows up occasionally in a punctuation which is dense and little orthodox, even by the standards of his time. The organisation of Smith's major works does not follow any discernible system. 'Books', 'chapters', 'sections', 'parts', 'articles', 'introductions' and 'conclusions' alternate without any systemic ambition. Their length and the number of textual hierarchies vary greatly according to the need of the specific argument being treated.

The work of Adam Smith resembles one of those fractal designs, where the same figure is repeated from the smallest to the largest scale, thus creating an image that is utterly devoid of any linear system and yet displays a profound coherence. This essay about the structure, the informational assumptions and the ethical aspirations of Adam Smith's work draws the attention of the reader to its singularity and even strangeness, in order to better understand the ongoing fascination it exerts and to appreciate the lasting importance that it still has today. The objective is to allow us to regard the original texts with a fresh view. We propose a new reading of the work of Adam Smith

1.2 An economy of the passions in a double system of coordinates

Such a new reading requires clear indications in order to avoid being distracted either by the multiple secondary threads weaving themselves through the central narrative of the work or by the cacophony of voices surrounding it. To facilitate orientation, it is best to reveal the principal argument immediately. Without further ado, we will thus present, in the following, the central theses of this essay, foregoing the usual preliminaries concerning the general importance of the work and the respect we owe to the man, founder of a new discipline, which a more complete work would have required.[1]

The Theory of Moral Sentiments, the first major work that Adam Smith published in 1759, relies on *two* different processes (which are, as we will show further below, orthogonal to each other) to generate normative rules of behaviour. Both of these processes will remain identifiable, although in different forms, in *The Wealth of Nations*. The first process is well known, even though its implications, in particular its implications for the working of a market economy, have not always been fully grasped. This is the 'sympathy mechanism', a self-reinforcing feedback process through which the individual seeks the recognition of his own feelings by his peers, as well as the identification of their feelings within himself. This process is ultimately founded on the need to feel liked and even loved. The phrase 'humanity does not desire to be great, but to be beloved' (Smith 1759 (III.5.8): 194) expresses perfectly this essential motivation of human behaviour according to Adam Smith.[2]

While the sympathy process is treated regularly in the secondary literature, with more or less precision, the second process capable of setting behavioural standards is evoked by commentators more sparingly. This second process is concerned with the development of a personal ethic, defined by the desire to do 'good' and to act in a just and virtuous manner. It relies heavily on individual introspection, structured around the notion of an abstract authority with divine characteristics – the 'impartial spectator'. This figure of the impartial spectator is present in the work of Adam Smith under a multitude of designations, such as the 'great judge', 'the Director of nature', 'the demigod within the breast' and many others. This proliferation of the names of the impartial spectator will in itself be a theme for discussion further on.

To facilitate the representation of these two processes, one may associate the first process with a horizontal dimension referring to notions of equality, of the market and of lateral communication. One may associate the second process with a vertical dimension referring to notions of authority, of hierarchy and of communication between different levels. Inspite of certain attempts to link them and certain contact points, the two processes are essentially incompatible and are presented as such by the author of the *Theory of Moral Sentiments*. Each one of the two processes constructs a distinct set of rules capable of generating a system of coherent behaviour with clearly identified objectives. Adam Smith himself expresses the incompatibility of the two processes the following way:

> In estimating our own merit, in judging of our own character and conduct, there are two different standards to which we naturally compare them. The one is the idea of exact propriety and perfection … The other is that degree of approximation to this idea which is commonly attained in the world, and in which the greater part of our friends, and companions, of our rivals and competitors, may have actually arrived at … The wise and virtuous man directs his principal attention to the first standard … It is the slow, gradual, and progressive work of the great demigod within the breast, the great judge and arbiter of conduct.
>
> (Smith 1759 (VI.3.23–25): 291–92)

At the beginning of the book, he had already underlined in a more general manner:

> To deserve, to acquire, and to enjoy the respect and admiration of mankind, are the great objects of ambition and emulation. Two different roads are presented to us, equally leading to the attainment of this so much desired object; the one by the study of wisdom and the practice of virtue; the other, by the acquisition of wealth and greatness.
>
> (Smith 1759 (I.3.2): 73)

In both cases, Smith identifies as the force inciting individuals to follow one or the other of the two normative principles, the most intense of the human passions, that is 'to be beloved'. The subject of the thus desired love is, however, very different in each case. In the first case, the subjects of love are the 'others', the equals, the friends, the peers, the competitors, the neighbours, in short society. In the second case, it is the figure of the 'impartial spectator'. The desire to obtain the love, either of the 'impartial spectator' or of one's peers, is sufficiently strong to ensure the control of all other passions, which are considered as violent and as incompatible with social life. 'Self-control' is thus, according to Smith, an indispensable and highly prized virtue for the establishment of any sociability.

Adam Smith's entire project of exploring the forces that structure society begins with the question 'How can one control the violent passions in order to render social life possible?' Today, one would speak about 'impulses' rather than 'passions'. The fundamental problem is that of an innate and inevitable violence manifesting itself already in childhood, a condition that has been referred to for the past 100 years as the Oedipus complex. Adam Smith refers explicitly to the unfortunate king of Thebes, distinguishing however between his responsibility and his culpability, declaring him responsible but not guilty given that his crime was committed unconsciously, a distinction that is, as we shall see, crucial for Smith's concept of practical morality. One should not forget either that Adam Smith, the man, lost his father before birth and lived with his mother all his life, except for his last six years. The control of the passions was no anodyne subject for the professor of moral philosophy.

One needs to understand the parallel development of *two* competing mechanisms developing normative frameworks from the point of view that both serve to control the passions. In spite of their shared purpose, *The Theory of Moral Sentiments* shows that the two principles clash directly on the level of individual decision-making. At the end of *The Theory of Moral Sentiments*, two possible extensions thus present themselves. The first is a work on the auto-organisation of individuals culminating in a state whose normative justification is intrinsically linked to self-interested, individual decision-making based on the sympathy mechanism. The publication of *The Wealth of Nations* in 1776 masterfully realises this option. In Chapter 2 of this essay, 'Sympathy, communication, exchange – the horizontal world', we will analyse this first normative principle based on the sympathy mechanism in *The Theory of Moral Sentiments* and *The Wealth of Nations*. This, by the way, allows us to answer conclusively the question about the much discussed relationship between the two books: *The Wealth of Nations* constitutes a direct, but partial, extension of *The Theory of Moral Sentiments*.

We can only guess at the analogue development of the second option, although Adam Smith refers explicitly to it. At the end of *The Theory of Moral Sentiments*, he thus announces the forthcoming publication of a *History of Natural Jurisprudence*, which would explore a normative framework whose origins would be *exogenous* to the processes of individual decision-making by individuals. This announcement is maintained throughout all of the six editions published during his lifetime, even though Smith remarks in the foreword of the sixth edition of 1790, the year of his death, that the completion of this work is no longer on the agenda. Without disposing of the relevant textual evidence, we may legitimately suppose that this *History of Natural Jurisprudence* constitutes the second extension of *The Theory of Moral Sentiments*, the systematic development of a normative framework based not on the auto-organisation of individuals but on autonomous principles that, at the same time, are more universal and more personal, than the conventional decrees of society.

John Rae, Smith's biographer, tells us that a handwritten version of this *History of Natural Jurisprudence* was burned, by Smith's order, a few days before his death. In Chapter 3, 'The Vertical World of the Impartial Spectator', we will identify the principal characteristics of this second normative principle governed by the 'impartial spectator' and will explore its implications for the understanding of Adam Smith's complete work. Although *The Wealth of Nations* mainly develops the first principle, it contains clearly identifiable traces of the second principle, particularly in the passages concerning the notion of 'justice', which is closely associated with the 'impartial spectator'.

1.3 The horizontal principle: sympathy, exchange and the market

The Wealth of Nations provides us with a vision of a world built on a form of a shared rationality shaped by the sympathy mechanism. In Chapter 2, 'Sympathy, communication, exchange – the horizontal world' we will determine the nature of this rationality developed in *The Theory of Moral Sentiments*, where it is opposed to an individually defined ethic structured by the impartial spectator. We will see that this 'rational sympathy' is at the origin of the notion of a socially determined 'self-interest'. This notion of a self-interest *formatted* by social processes (in the literal sense of shaping it into a specific form) is at the heart of Smith's theory of society, and later, of the economy. It receives its logical coherence and theoretical tractability through the chronological separation of the process of preference formation, based on social processes, and the actions based on these preferences, which are individual.

The detailed rendering of these individual actions based on the 'values' established by the sympathy mechanism is the great theme of *The Wealth of Nations*. It thus advances the investigation of this important aspect of *The Theory of Moral Sentiments*. (Some of the misunderstanding of the work of Adam Smith stems from the fact that the readers of *The Wealth of Nations* look to *The Theory of Moral Sentiments* for further detail and precision. Instead, they only find far broader preparatory deliberations.) All the while, self-interest, the cornerstone of all human behaviour in *The Wealth of Nations*, remains closely linked to social functions. Not only has self-interest been structured by a process of social emulation, but it also preserves, from *The Theory of Moral Sentiments*, a double teleology: wealth acquisition is but a means to a higher appreciation by one's peers and, as is well known, realises general welfare in the process.

With Adam Smith there is never a contradiction between the pursuit of this self-interest, which is very specific and highly codified, and sociability. On the contrary, we shall see that the adoption of this self-interest, as opposed to the anarchic expression of one's untutored passions, is the very basis of social life. The formation of first general, then economic, values through the sympathy mechanism and the behaviour that stems from them eventually *creates* the system of social organisation we call a 'market society' today. A liberal economic order is for Smith not an assumption formulated a priori. It is the result of a wide-ranging exploration of the anthropological and psychological determinants that allow social life to arise and to prosper.

The transformation of a world ruled by the desire to be loved by one's peers into a system of markets is accomplished by the radical reduction (ultimately, elimination) of all informational transaction costs. This reduction is due to the qualitative standardisation, the codification, of preferences. The establishment of an unbreakable link between all goods and their 'value' allows the establishment of a pervasive system of exchanges, which evolves into a system of competitive markets in *The Wealth of Nations* (see section 2.2). This freezing of the informational units ensures, together with the division of labour (which depends in itself on this codification) and the vigorous rejection of all forms of economic monopoly, a structure of production that is characterised by constant returns to scale and establishes perfect competition as the horizon of the economic process.

Just like submitting to the demands of the impartial spectator, economic behaviour based on the sympathy mechanism is part of a larger concern, the control of the original, egoistical and antisocial passions. In a paradoxical manner one may say that, for Adam Smith, self-interest, as long as it is shaped by the sympathy mechanism, guarantees the social bond. Contrary to a generally accepted idea, the *homo œconomicus* is an intensely social being (see sections 2.2 and 3.2).

The image of the invisible hand starts from the same paradox and pushes it even further. The sympathy mechanism turns socially harmful individual 'passions' into 'sentiments' that can be shared and into a desire for social recognition through the acquisition of wealth and hence engagement in economic activity. Together, these two processes form the foundations of social life. Based on these foundations, the invisible hand will ensure the realisation of general welfare, for which the control of the passions is a necessary but insufficient condition. For example, following the injunctions of the impartial spectator equally ensures the control of the passions, but it is unable to guarantee general welfare despite the fact that the latter is explicitly part of his objectives.

In '"Efficient causes" and "final causes": the working of the invisible hand' in Chapter 4, the precise function of the image of the invisible hand will be examined. Contrary to what is implied by its numerous metaphorical interpretations, the invisible hand introduces no exogenous, additional elements into the economic system devised by Smith. This system, based on the preferences shaped by the mechanism of sympathy, not only allows, but *implies*, the achievement of general well-being. Economic order and general welfare are the inevitable consequences of the initial conditions defined by the sympathy mechanism and the desire to be loved: the codification of preferences, the division of labour and consequently, competitive markets. These three initial conditions, however, are not of the same logical order. We will see below how the codification of preferences, through the sympathy mechanism, will enable the division of labour and will thus prepare for the elimination of monopolies and the establishment of competitive markets.

The alignment of individual interest and general interest thus proceeds according to a prior and deep-seated design, which is part of human nature and its desire for social participation, and not according to a new, supplementary design, which was added *ex post*. We will see that in Adam Smith's work, all the conditions for the concurrence of individual and general interest are already given with the peculiar informational structure that determines individual behaviour.

This logically inevitable, and hence automatic, convergence of the pursuit of private profit and general welfare is protected rather than created by the invisible hand. In the pursuit of its function, the invisible hand does not add anything to the behaviour of the individual agents interested only in maximising their wealth. Instead, it removes something. The invisible hand removes the agent's knowledge of the original plan of the 'Director of nature', in which he is taking part. This ignorance ensures that he will not perturb the deployment of the socially beneficial programme inscribed in his socially constructed selfishness. The invisible hand is not only invisible itself. It also *veils*, renders invisible, the existence of the creator and his plans. This removes the danger of a direct pursuit of the latter's objectives through misplaced ambition driven by speculative thinking, which according to Adam Smith is always a perturbing influence.

The invisible hand thus guarantees that the intrinsic qualities of the behaviour defined by the horizontal principle of the sympathy mechanism can flourish without hindrance. Paradoxically – and this paradox is at the very foundation of Smith's teleology – the very limitation of any direct influence of the impartial spectator guarantees the achievement of his original design of general welfare (see also Chapter 4, 'The paradoxical synthesis').

1.4 The vertical principle: the impartial spectator

Throughout the text of *The Theory of Moral Sentiments*, a second process capable of establishing norms of human behaviour weaves its way in counterpoint. This second process no longer originates in the inter-subjective relationships between individuals of equal standing. It constructs itself on the basis of individual introspection, philosophical cogitation and the study of historical examples. This process and the values and norms it establishes all revolve around a figure that is conventionally referred to as the 'impartial spectator', although Adam Smith rarely uses this expression. Those values imply *ethical* actions which will find approval in the eyes of a superior authority independently of – and sometimes in contradiction to – the social values established by the sympathy mechanism. Adam Smith underlines throughout *The Theory of Moral Sentiments* that men find themselves constantly in conflict between the noble pursuit of the expectations of this higher authority and the temptation to abandon oneself to comfortable sociability established by the sympathy mechanism.

As much as Adam Smith is adamant about the existence of this second principle, he is vague about its precise nature. This explains, in part, the difficulty that many commentators have to accord the impartial spectator the status of an autonomous normative reference. The choice of the appellation 'impartial spectator', whose continued use in this essay is only justified by its historical role, is in itself a sign of this difficulty. Chapter 3 of this book, 'The vertical world of the mpartial spectator', shows to what extent the expression 'impartial spectator' is a source of misunderstanding and presents the long list of alternative titles that Adam Smith employs to designate this higher authority. These expressions make various references to a divine presence, a paternal function or an undisputable higher Law. The difficulty of finding a definitive name for this entity that combines features of god, conscience or a father-figure, with which the Smithian individual maintains a constant interior dialogue, is part of the defining aspects of *The Theory of Moral Sentiments.*

Contrary to the values established by the sympathy mechanism, the values established in the interior dialogue with the impartial spectator are not codifiable. They vacillate between highly abstract aspirations – the common good, social utility – and perfectly individual ones defined by a person's history and character. They provide a personal identity rather than a socially recognised position. On the level of his psychological economy, an individual searching to satisfy the expectations of the impartial spectator is looking for inner peace and an identity based on universal ethical principles.

Adam Smith stages the conflict between the two principles throughout the better part of *The Theory of Moral Sentiments.* This conflict arrives at a culminating point when he evokes the notion of 'moral sense' developed by his professor, mentor and predecessor at the chair of moral philosophy of the University of Glasgow, Francis Hutcheson.

Following an enthusiastic, but general eulogy of his contribution, Smith mercilessly deconstructs the pertinence of the notion of 'moral sense' and ultimately rejects its existence (see section 3.1 'The names of Adam's father: looking for the impartial spectator').

However, the function of Hutcheson's concept of moral sense was precisely to provide the ability to sustain the interior dialogue with the impartial spectator, to be able to distinguish between 'right' and 'wrong', independently of social conventions. Moral sense is supposed to be innate and independent of any social intermediation. Refusing Hutcheson's concept, the principal mode of communication with the impartial spectator, Adam Smith, relegates the vertical principle to second place behind the horizontal principle organised by the sympathy mechanism. This relegation was prepared, albeit in less drastic form, in the discussion of the 'two tribunals'. The 'tribunal of intentions', which is presided over by the impartial spectator, is considered to be the highest in principle; for all practical purposes, however, the 'tribunal of men', which judges only verifiable facts, is the only competent institution to judge human affairs in everyday life (see section 3.1).

And yet, a residual of the vertical principle and the demands of the impartial spectator survive in the notion of 'justice', and this in both *The Theory of Moral Sentiments* as well as in *The Wealth of Nations.* 'Justice', which is always administered by the state, never by the market, is for Adam Smith a defensive notion, defined more easily by its absence, which implies a state of lawless chaos, rather than by its presence '… the violation of justice is what men will never submit to from one another' (Smith 1759 (VII.IV.36): 402). The rules of justice have no positive content and thus cannot by themselves constitute a complete normative framework for human behaviour. Instead, they provide and protect the space in which such frameworks can develop. Adam Smith compares them to the laws of grammar which are necessary to write correctly but are insufficient to write well:

> There is, however, one virtue of which the general rules determine with the greatest exactness every external action which it requires. This virtue is justice … The rules of justice may be compared to the rules of grammar; the rules of the other virtues, to the rules which critics lay down for the attainment of what is sublime and elegant in composition. The one, are precise, accurate, and indispensable. The other are loose, vague and indeterminate …
>
> (Smith 1759 (III.6.10–11): 203–5)

The very precision of the rules of justice demands that they be void of any positive content. Submitting to justice alone can never suffice for the organisation of social life, for which justice is a necessary but not a sufficient condition. Once the vertical principle has been rejected, the horizontal principle with its gradual convergence towards shared values through reciprocal observation will thus remain indispensable to establish a complete framework for human behaviour.

1.5 The paradoxical synthesis

The eviction of the impartial spectator and the establishment of the sympathy mechanism as the principal regulatory principle of social life at the end of *The Theory of Moral Sentiments* are confirmed in *The Wealth of Nations*, where all human action reposes on values based exclusively on generalised social approbation. Section 2.2 will show how the sympathy mechanism sets in motion a highly specific process of preference formation, which in turn is decisive for the formation of a market society. Attempts to identify a contradiction between the market-oriented behaviour presented in *The Wealth of Nations* and the notion of sympathy are inevitably the result of a superficial reading of *The Theory of Moral Sentiments* (see also later the comments on 'das Adam Smith Problem').

The elimination of the impartial spectator as a directly active force in the regulation of human affairs should not be seen as a peaceful succession of different normative principles, both of which aim at the control of socially harmful passions. On the contrary, one principle is substituted for another, which is diametrically opposed to the first. Nor is Adam Smith passing from a general discussion of social life, characterised by the active presence of the impartial spectator to the specific discussion of economic life, which would be characterised by his absence, as maintained by Daniel Diatkine, for example (Diatkine 1991: 28). Smith's own style is, in fact characterised by an unusual verbal violence when he refutes Hutcheson's notion of 'moral sense', which was the principal channel of communication with the impartial spectator.

The exclusive dominance of the horizontal principle based on the sympathy mechanism that follows from this operation is a general phenomenon, which is not restricted to any specific area of social life such as economics. Adam Smith rather elevates a form of interaction that lends itself naturally to the establishment of a market society to an *exclusive* form of social interaction thus 'economising' the whole of society. The radical nature and the specificity of Smith's approach are precisely based on the theoretical motivation of the all-pervasiveness of the sympathy mechanism whose essence is the exchange of looks, words, values and goods. Smith forcefully insists on the innate, unconscious and inevitable nature of the human tendency to engage in all forms of exchange as in the famous passage that introduces the division of labour:

> The division of labour, from which so many advantages are derived, is not originally the effect of any human wisdom, which foresees and intends the general opulence to which it gives occasion. It is the necessary … consequence of a certain propensity in human nature … the propensity to truck, barter, and exchange one thing for another.
>
> (Smith 1776 (I.I.2): 17)

Adam Smith subsequently presents this inclination as a fundamental principle of human nature and as a consequence of the capacity to think and speak. The quoted passage underlines the fact that the benefits derived from the propensity to exchange are not a consciously formulated objective but the result of abandoning oneself to a constant of human nature. This is a theme Adam Smith comes back to repeatedly, occasionally underlining the benefits of a certain ignorance or intellectual modesty (see also Chapter 4 'The paradoxical synthesis'). This renouncement of an active, constructively creating approach to social matters is part and parcel of institutionalising market exchange as the predominant form of social interaction (see also section 2.2).

And yet, Adam Smith's final vision of society is far more sophisticated than an unconditional eulogy of the surviving normative framework, which we refer to as the horizontal principle. In fact, already throughout the text of *The Theory of Moral Sentiments*, the opposition between the two principles varies (see also Chapter 5 'The ethics of morality'). In particular cases, identical outcomes can even result from alternatively following one principle or the other, even though the structural incompatibility between the two is never in doubt:' … the virtues of prudence, justice and beneficence may, upon different occasions, be recommended to us almost equally by [the] two different principles' (Smith 1759 (VI.Conclusion.2): 310).

The particular role of justice in linking the two axes has already been mentioned. *The Wealth of Nations* also contains remnants of a world organised according to principles other than that of generalised market exchange (see, for instance, Smith's remarks concerning national defence, slavery or primary education). Most importantly, however, a market society ensures the attainment of the ultimate objective of the teleology structured around the impartial spectator – general welfare – and this far better than their direct pursuit would have ever permitted (see Chapter 4).[3]

At least in *The Theory of Moral Sentiments*, the notion of general welfare is closely linked to the 'propagation of the species'. While it may come as a surprise for an author associated with the benefits of the pursuit of individual self-interest, there can be no doubt that Smith frequently pursues a Darwinian logic, in which the survival and the well-being of the species, or of society as a whole, is of higher importance than the survival of the individual. General welfare and propagation of the species can be pursued following two different routes. The first would imply following the injunctions of the impartial spectator to pursue the common good after a preparatory phase of intense introspection. Following the second, indirect, route consists, of course, of letting oneself be guided by the sympathy mechanism. This second approach will usually function better, even though, or rather *because*, each individual believes subjectively to be working only for his own personal benefit (see Chapter 4 '"Efficient causes" and "final causes": the working of the invisible hand').

Paradoxically, the indirect route which relies on the sympathy mechanism to trigger the appropriate 'effective causes' is considered the safer choice for satisfying the ultimate objective of the impartial spectator. Trying to identify with the will of the Creator directly is perhaps a noble enterprise for small elites, but it is also a hazardous enterprise fraught with danger. Unmitigated and absolute adherence to the high demands of a divine authority can render one proud, exacting and asocial or even antisocial. Pursuing one's self-interest, as long as it has been formatted by social interaction, is far less risky, in particular for the great majority of average men. The common good is thus born from the naivety of men and their search for love in each other's complicit looks.

In *The Theory of Moral Sentiments*, pursuing the vertical orientation directly is still considered a noble choice for a small group of select men. In *The Wealth of Nations* this option is now firmly rejected as hypocritical and dangerous:

> By pursuing his own interest he [the individual] frequently promotes that of the society more effectually than when he really intends to promote it. I have never known much good done by those who affected to trade for the public good.
>
> (Smith 1776 (I.IV.2): 477)

It is the task of the invisible hand to organise this paradoxical logic: largely ignorant individuals who subjectively pursue their self-interest, having liberated themselves from the direct imperatives of the impartial spectator, objectively ensure the common good and thus the impartial spectator's most important objective. Men thus remain guided by their desire to be loved, their thirst for social recognition that derives from it and hence the drive to maximise their wealth, which remains the surest way to gain the esteem of one's peers.

The codification of their preferences through the sympathy mechanism ensures that their actions, which can be characterised with the help of a small number of parameters, are compatible. This in return ensures the form of highly developed auto-organisation typical of economic equilibria. Maximising their own profits, men thus promote a general economic well-being, which plays no role in their calculations (see Chapter 4 '"Efficient Causes" and "Final Causes": The Working of the Invisible Hand').

1.6 The stakes of a well-established problem – das Adam Smith problem

The sophistication and originality of Adam Smith's approach owe more to his capacity to sustain a tension between opposing poles than to any systematic linear development of a single unified proposition. This sophistication has occasionally induced even the most diligent readers to identify contradictions in Smith's work (less diligent readers content themselves with a partial reading that satisfies their a priori prejudices). A typical example of the first type of reading is the careful and well-documented study by François Dermange, *Le Dieu du Marché*. Dermange in fact concludes with the failure of Adam Smith's philosophical project, which he claims to have consisted of unifying economic behaviour with a moral aspiration. Having been unable to find effective and appropriate moral imperatives capable of putting limits to economic behaviour, Smith supposedly abandoned his project and concentrated thereafter only on economics (Dermange 2003: 15, 186 and 198).

In broader terms, Albert Otto Hirschman had already said that Smith's 'proposition [that the pursuit of personal interest contributes to general welfare] turned out to be riddled with so many intellectual puzzles that sorting and solving them occupied generations of economists (Hirschman 1997: 112). Even Jean-Pierre Dupuy, perhaps the most profoundly innovative contributor to the secondary literature on Adam Smith in recent years, is not above identifying 'contradictions' in

Smith's work after having rejected his key notion of the social function of wealth (Dupuy 1992: 98).

Generally speaking, the venerable notion of an *Adam Smith Problem* refers to the fact that commentators find it difficult to establish one linear sense in Adam Smith's work. The diligent, if uninspired, German university professors of the second half of the nineteenth century who coined the now standard expression were the first to realise that searching for one single development in *The Theory of Moral Sentiments* and *The Wealth of Nations* posed a number of questions. Since then many contributions to the secondary literature have placed themselves, implicitly or explicitly, in a perspective of providing an ongoing commentary to the *Adam Smith Problem*.

However, identifying a 'failure' or a 'contradiction' in the wake of a renewed setback following the attempt to find a single unified proposition in Smith's work contains its own implicit contradictions. If the failure in question is really the result of a logical inconsistency or another major flaw in the argument, how then does one explain Adam Smith's singular position in the history of ideas? One does not build a new discipline and a formidable intellectual influence on intellectual failure or on 'contradictions', except, of course, if they are made fertile in the sense of a dialectical process. One does not discuss for 250 years a non-issue. Even the most aggressive critics bear witness to the ongoing attention consecrated to the work, the man and the myth for over 200 years. Each contradiction they identify is a proof of the continuing force and interest of the ideas they are trying to neutralise.

Yet an essay on the history of thought needs not only to defend the interest of its subject but also needs to go beyond a 'Darwinist' approach, in the sense that every piece of thought that succeeds in retaining the attention of a sufficient number of commentators is necessarily coherent. This contribution strives to show that the paradoxical structure of Adam Smith's work not only corresponds to a coherent project of its author but is also responsible for the intense interest of successive generations of readers. This paradoxical structure is based on the conflict between the two normative principles that structure *The Theory of Moral Sentiments*, the socialising force of the sympathy mechanism and the loyalty to objectives of the impartial spectator.

Adam Smith's project comes to fruition with the paradoxical synthesis provided in *The Wealth of Nations*. The paradox consists of the fact that the normative principle which dominates at the end of *The Theory of Moral Sentiments* and which determines the microstructure of human behaviour in *The Wealth of Nations* is ultimately used to advance the objectives of the alternative principle, which had been discarded as a directly active influence on human behaviour. The paradox thus resolves into an intricate synthesis, which is more than a simple compromise, since both principles remain fully distinct and fully realised, albeit on different levels of the argument.

The extraordinary fertility of 'das Adam Smith Problem' stems primarily from the desire of readers to find *one* single, linear argument per book and the fact that this desire is necessarily thwarted given that each work elaborates distinct partial aspects of the double structure, which dominates them both. The naïve idea that Adam Smith simply renounced *The Theory of Moral Sentiments* to write *The Wealth of Nations* is untenable. On the biographical level, Adam Smith continued working on his first published work well after the publication of *The Wealth of Nations.* The sixth and last version of *The Theory of Moral Sentiments* that includes major revisions dates from 1790, the year of his death.

At the level of the texts there is no contradiction between the two books but a double development common to both, of which each book elaborates different aspects. On the one hand, there is solid continuity between the two as the sympathy mechanism provides the preference structure at the basis of the economic behaviour spelled out in *The Wealth of Nations.* This process of social communication is motivated by the emotional need of each individual to recognise himself and his feelings in those of his peers in order to satisfy his 'desire to be loved'. On the other hand, the impartial spectator who had an important and explicit role in *The Theory of Moral Sentiments* has almost no active part in *The Wealth of Nations*, where he is present only behind the scenes as the 'Director of nature' who put the determinants of human behaviour in place and defined the basic teleology of the work – the achievement of general welfare. The solution to the *Adam Smith Problem* is thus the following: given that the two normative principles that were opposed in *The Theory of Moral Sentiments* are taken up in a strongly differentiated manner in *The Wealth of Nations*, the latter is the direct but partial continuation of the former.

Adam Smith himself highlights this continuity when he notes in the foreword to the sixth edition of *The Theory of Moral Sentiments* that *The Wealth of Nations* had kept the promise made at the end of the first edition of *The Theory of Moral Sentiments* to develop an account of the general principles of government regarding civil justice, taxes and defence. The fact that this continuity develops on two different levels – the level of the motivations and the underlying economy of the passions on the one hand and the level of the resulting actions or facts on the other – does not prevent characterising this continuity precisely.

Bringing out the internal coherence of Smith's work, and with it the absence of major contradictions, does not, obviously, do away with the need to continue questioning its specific hypotheses and underlying assumptions. To give but one example: concerning the sympathy mechanism, the neat separation in time between the formation of preferences and their realisation in economic action that Smith presupposes seems empirically difficult to justify. (On this point see later section 3.2 where we discuss Adam Smith's theory that the first manifestations of the sympathy mechanism take place at a very young age in primary school). Despite his great diligence, the author Adam Smith occasionally displays a certain predilection for formulaic expressions which underline the paradoxical character of his approach while concealing the links between different statements. Notwithstanding, it is possible to show clearly the fundamental coherence of his vast project of translating the results of a philosophical inquiry into the anthropological and psychological bases of life in society into a theory of economic exchange and auto-organisation.

Ultimately however, the 'genius' of Adam Smith, his singular contribution guaranteeing his place in the history of ideas, does not reside in the diligent elaboration of this project but in the synthesis of the two normative principles, structured by the sympathy mechanism and the impartial spectator respectively, which he establishes. This synthesis is not realised on the basis of an arbitrary mix of ethical directives and explicit interdictions stemming from both principles in equal manner. Such a middling solution would have satisfied many of the critics discovering 'contradictions' in Adam Smith's work. Exogenous interdictions are neither necessary nor useful in a Smithian world, once the direct role of the impartial spectator has been terminated. The unassuming pursuit of a kind of self-interest shaped by social processes and in scrupulous observance of the laws of the land will realise all the objectives associated with the ethical authority embodied by the impartial spectator. One cannot emphasise strongly enough the fact that the self-interest of the Smithian individual, which is the expression of the original passions transformed into socially acceptable sentiments, is a very particular and highly codified self-interest. This process is the great theme of *The Theory of Moral Sentiments.* Ultimately, the pursuit of this highly formatted self-interest *must* attain general welfare. Revealing the sophistication and profoundness of this operation is a key ambition of this essay.[4]

Last but not least, the difficulties of interpreting Smith's work results also from the disciplinary issue at stake. Given that the most advanced expression of this work is *The Wealth of Nations*, it is natural that economists should be amongst those primarily interested. Given its origins in *The Theory of Moral Sentiments* it is equally natural that historians of thought and philosophers have studied it and commented on it. The contingencies of the different fields of research have often helped little to advance the understanding of the links that Adam Smith constructed between the two worlds. Economists usually approach *The Theory of Moral Sentiments* after having read *The Wealth of Nations*. As a result of their economic training, they take as given the specific mental and emotional processes, which establish the peculiar modes of thinking and communicating that define market society. Discovering the problematic development of these modes of reasoning and communicating in the tension between contrasting normative references usually provokes more puzzlement and questions than satisfying answers. On the other hand, historians of thought have often been unconcerned about the formal implications that result from Smith's conclusions and are content to pursue partial enquiries of textual and historical references.

It is, however, the *linking* of a model of human psychology and the highly codified individual behaviour that results from it with a social teleology which is the most original and influential contribution of Adam Smith. The connection between these poles is ensured by a model of communication and social interaction, whose psychological, moral and ethical foundations are explored in *The Theory of Moral Sentiments* and whose economic, political and social implications are explored in *The Wealth of Nations*.

This model is based on the clear separation in time of the formation of preferences and their realisation in economic activity and the potential for static codification that such a separation permits. Adopting it, economic science began to gain its autonomy from the other social sciences. The process of ever greater autonomy was driven by the gradual advancement of technical and mathematical sophistication and abstraction, with which economists have carried on the work and spirit of Adam Smith. The fact that the analysis of behaviour, which we refer to today as 'economic', ultimately takes a dominant place in this work is not due to a wanton choice after the conclusion of his first book. The study of economic behaviour is the inevitable consequence of the development of a precise model of social interaction that implies economic behaviour as a particular form of social behaviour.

'The coherence of Adam Smith's work reveals itself in the continuous interest in this "propensity of human nature" to exchange and communicate of which he speaks at the beginning of *The Wealth of Nations*' (Smith 1776 (I.I.2): 17). The exchange of goods remains in its structure and implications the direct consequence of the exchange of the looks, sentiments and values that Adam Smith presents in *The Theory of Moral Sentiments* An act of exchange always supposes the coincidence of two mental universes around a given notion of value, which is precisely the result an individual participating in the sympathy mechanism hopes for. Adam Smith's vast and lasting influence ultimately relies on the profound coherence of the universe he proposes: the benefits of a distinct form of social organisation based on competitive markets are the originally aimed-for result of a comprehensive deliberation about human psychology, communication, social interaction, morality and ethics.

2 Sympathy, communication, exchange

The horizontal world

2.1 Self-interest in the service of sociability: the world of sympathy

The exchange of looks

No reader of *The Theory of Moral Sentiments* can overlook the sympathy mechanism which is presented with force and clarity at the very beginning of the book. It establishes a central theme in the long reflections that follow about the conflict between the ethical obligations emanating from the impartial spectator and the behaviour suggested by a set of more conventional moral injunctions. Adam Smith's remarks about the sympathy mechanism are straightforward and precise. This, however, does not mean that their implications – in particular their implications for the development of an autonomous theory of economic behaviour with scientific aspirations – have always been fully grasped.[1]

The sympathy mechanism is, in fact, at the origin of the formation of an *economic rationality*. Once this fact is understood, the internal coherence of Smith's oeuvre becomes apparent. The sympathy mechanism creates this economic rationality by codifying in a reciprocal social process a system of values, preferences and intentions that permits the organisation of coherent and consistent individual actions in the light of one single, explicit objective – the maximisation of individual wealth. Each and every action contributing to utility maximisation must beforehand pass the test of that inter-subjective process which is the sympathy mechanism.

To clarify one thing once and for all: sympathy is not altruism. It is in fact quite far from it. First of all, sympathy is a *positive* notion and not a *normative* one. The normative notion of altruism is called 'beneficence' by Smith and is orthogonal to sympathy in the sense that its observation is implied by a radically different normative reference. Beneficence is, in fact, closely associated with the impartial spectator (see Chapter 4.1 '"Efficient causes" and "final causes": the working of the invisible hand') and plays no role in establishing the pleasing concurrence of feelings between equals, which is at the heart of the sympathy mechanism.

The horizontal sympathy mechanism organises the mutual perceptions between peers, neighbours or friends, all of whom are characterised by their 'likeness' to each other. The image of the mirror that Smith uses to symbolise the relation between the individual and the society that surrounds it, perfectly captures this reciprocal formation of one individual's preferences by those of the 'others', who do the same with him. Concerning an individual having grown up outside of civilised society Smith says, for instance 'Bring him into society, and he is immediately provided with the mirror which he wanted before' (Smith 1759 (III.I.3): 129).[2]

The visual perception of the other (the peer, the neighbour, the friend, the equal, the competitor …), which works like a mirror image, serves as a point of reference for the Smithian individual, who knows no other way to establish his own identity. An identical mechanism was later theorised under the heading of the 'stage of the mirror' (*stade de miroir*) by the French psychoanalyst Jacques Lacan. In connection with a theory of the establishment of the self, Lacan maintains that children in their narcissistic phase develop a sense of their unity and their own ego with the help of their own mirror image (Lacan 1966). This mechanism is doubled and reinforced by the perception of other children who are 'like me'.

Adam Smith offers us a first, very far-reaching version of this theory of the 'stage of the mirror'. In fact, all sentiments of pleasure or displeasure the Smithian individual may feel must first pass the test of whether other people around him have the same feelings. Sentiments or feelings always require reciprocal verification through the sympathy mechanism. The sensation of 'sympathy' thus remains for Adam Smith the precondition for any emotional reaction a well-socialised individual would allow himself. And sympathy is that pleasant feeling which arises when one discovers one's own sentiments in others:

> In every passion of which the mind of man is susceptible, the emotions of the bystander always correspond to what, by bringing the case home to himself, he imagines what should be the sentiments of the sufferer … Sympathy … may now, without much

> impropriety, be made use of to denote our fellow-feeling with any passion whatever.
>
> (Smith 1759 (I.I.1.4–5): 13)

The impetus to search for this harmony of sentiments springs from the desire to be understood, accepted and loved – the ultimate motor of human actions for Adam Smith. One's pleasure is thus primarily provided by the discovery that others have sentiments identical or at least similar to ours, since this is the precondition for any appreciative feelings they may have for us:

> But whatever may be the cause of sympathy, or however it may be excited, nothing pleases us more than to observe in other men a fellow-feeling with all the emotions of our own breast
>
> (Smith 1759 (I.I.2.1): 17)

Sympathy and the harmonisation of perceptions

The pleasure to be had from the feeling of mutual sympathy is considerable, yet it is not easy to come by. The reason is the following. An individual's feelings, or sentiments as Smith would have called them, originate in final instance from his inner 'passions'. Yet unadulterated passions are asocial for Adam Smith and due to their intrinsic violence even antisocial (see section 3.2). The original feelings based on individual passions thus need to be transformed into *sentiments* that one can communicate and share, which demands a strong and sustained effort of self-education and moderation. The original passions or impulses need to be made communicable, which renders their momentum orthogonal to its original direction. The 'vertical' passions are thus transformed into 'horizontal' sentiments, which can be fed into a process of establishing sympathy between similar individuals.

The control and transformation of the original passions are indispensable to be able to participate in the sympathy mechanism. This is a hard and laborious process. Achieving perfect sympathy remains an ideal to strive for rather than a daily reality:

> Mankind, though naturally sympathetic, never conceive, for what has befallen another, that degree of passion which naturally animates the person principally concerned … The person principally concerned is sensible of this, and at the same time passionately

> desires a more complete sympathy … To see the emotions of their hearts, in every respect, beat time to his own, in the violent and disagreeable passions constitutes his sole consolation. But he can only hope to obtain this by lowering his passion to that pitch, in which the spectators are capable of going along with him. He must flatten, if I may be allowed to say so, the sharpness of its natural tone, in order to reduce it to harmony and concord with the emotions of those who are about him. What they feel will, indeed, always be, in some respects, different from what he feels, and compassion can never be exactly the same with the original sorrow … These two sentiments, however, may, it is evident, have such a correspondence with one another, as is sufficient for the harmony of society. Though they will never be unisons, they may be concords, and this is all that is wanted or required.
>
> (Smith 1759 (I.I.4.7): 26–27)

In the passage just cited Adam Smith seems to indicate that establishing sympathy, so to say, only requires the *qualitative* harmonisation of the sentiments of various agents. That is, sympathy would only require that the feelings of the various participants be on the same 'wavelength' as other universally recognised and communicable sentiments attached to the same arguments. As in music, it would not be necessary for two notes to be identical (unison) to create a harmonious accord. The sentiments and perceptions established by the sympathy mechanism need to become 'isomorphic' to use the expression of Jean-Pierre Dupuy.

The relevant analogy in economic theory would be a demand curve where the various preferences for a given good are all organised in the same price – quantity plane. The qualitative specification of preferences would be common to all, without these preferences needing to be of an identical quantitative measure. Other passages in *The Theory of Moral Sentiments*, however, go further and require precisely the quantitative harmonisation that was not considered indispensable in the passage quoted above. In this second case, the transformation of the original feelings must be advanced until it achieves the perfect coincidence of sentiments in both quality and quantity. At that point, a common interpersonal value is achieved that has the potential to establish a new social norm (propriety):

> The propriety of every passion excited by objects peculiarly related to ourselves, the pitch which the spectator can go along with, must

> lie, it is evident, in a certain mediocrity … This mediocrity … in which the point of propriety consists …
>
> (Smith 1759 (I.II.1–2): 32)

The term 'mediocrity' is not at all derogatory. For the very Aristotelian Adam Smith mediocrity is a quality of virtue itself:

> Virtue, according to Aristotle, consists in the habit of mediocrity according to right reason … It is unnecessary to observe that this account of virtue corresponds too pretty exactly with what has been said above concerning the propriety and impropriety of conduct.
>
> (Smith 1759 (VII.II.1.11): 319)

The mediocrity of sentiments does not result from lack of care or weakness. On the contrary, it is the fruit of the sustained effort to project oneself into the imagined perception that one's peers might have of oneself. The mutual reflection that results from this effort will transform the original incommunicable *passions* into universally accessible *sentiments*:

> In order to produce this concord, as nature teaches the spectators to assume the circumstances of the person principally concerned, so she teaches this last in some measure to assume those of the spectators … As their sympathy makes them look at it, in some measure, with his eyes, so his sympathy makes him look at it, in some measure, with theirs, especially when in their presence and acting under their observation: and as the reflected passion, which he thus conceives, is much weaker than the original one, it necessarily abates the violence of what he felt before he came into their presence, before he began to recollect in what manner they would be affected by it, and to view his situation in this candid and impartial light.
>
> (Smith 1759 (I.I.4.8): 27)

In the spectral virtuality of this mutual reflection the passions lose their original dangerousness. Completing the sympathy process requires self-control and the adaptation of one's passions to a middling level that can be grasped and shared by all. 'Propriety' and 'prudence' thus become the cardinal virtues of the Smithian individual since they are most apt to further such self-control. The desire to be loved – which is temporarily satisfied if the sympathy process is successfully completed – is so strong that the individual identifies himself completely with the supposed sentiments of his peers. References outside of the social values conveyed through the sympathy mechanism simply cease to exist. Jean-Pierre Dupuy formulated the implications of this state of affairs in the following way:

> You sympathise with yourself only to the precise degree that the others sympathise with you. In other words, you love yourself only to the precise degree that the others love you.
>
> (Dupuy 1988: 81, our translation)

The limits of sympathy

Despite its power and despite the important benefits it is able to generate – be it at the level of the individual or at the level of society as a whole – the sympathy mechanism never works automatically. It is a precious achievement, which always remains exposed to destabilising forces. It demands constant effort to make two mental universes coincide, which are a priori alien to each other. The 'mediocrity' of sentiments, the linear combination of two interior worlds, needs to overcome the double challenge of the muteness of the passions and the personal isolation of each individual that stems from them. This isolation is never overcome completely, as direct communication about one's inner state is impossible. Smith states somewhat bleakly:

> Every faculty in one man is the measure by which he judges of the like faculty in another. I judge of your sight by my sight, of your ear by my ear, of your reason by my reason, of your resentment by my resentment, of your love by my love. I neither have, nor can have any other way of judging about them.
>
> (Smith 1759 (I.I.3.10): 23)

The very positive view that Adam Smith holds of the role of exchange and commerce stems also from his pessimism concerning the existence of an easy and natural sociability allowing a more direct communication of the original, unadulterated passions.

Preparing oneself for the process of sympathy requires first of all the control of one's own original sentiments or passions. Of course, the sympathy mechanism will further the convergence of the sentiments of different individuals, but these will always be *derived* sentiments, or 'secondary' sentiments as Adam Smith calls them, shaped by self-control, which remains the basis of all sociability:

> The man of the most perfect virtue, the man whom we naturally love and revere the most, is he who joins, to the most perfect command of his own original and selfish feelings, the most exquisite sensibility both to the original and sympathetic feelings of others.
>
> (Smith 1759 (III.3.35): 176)

Note the difference! 'Original' feelings need to be distinguished from 'sympathetic' feelings. In the process of establishing mutual sympathy, which is the only means for social communication, there is no autonomous role for original, untransformed feelings, which Smith characterises here and elsewhere as 'selfish'. The latter include, in particular, all the feelings linked to physical sensations. Physical passions always constitute for Adam Smith a dangerous threat to the social bond. Only mediated and communicable passions are socially acceptable:

> And this [absence of sympathy] is the case of all the passions which take their origin from the body: they excite either no sympathy at all, or such a degree of it, as is altogether disproportioned to what is felt by the sufferer.
>
> (Smith 1759 (I.II.1.5): 35)

Adam Smith speaks briefly about sexual desire ('the passion that unites the sexes'), without prudishness but also without enthusiasm. Given that this particular passion is primarily a physical phenomenon, it remains incommunicable and is thus lost for establishing general sociability. For Smith, spectators in the theatre can therefore feel no sympathy for Phaedra's passion for her stepson Hippolyte in Racine's eponymous tragedy. Her *original* passion is not communicable. They can exclusively sympathise with Phaedra's *derived* passions, her social passions: her fear, her shame, her regret, her horror and her despair. Smith calls these 'the secondary passions … which arise from the situation of love' (Smith 1759 (I.II.2.4): 40).

Contrary to appearances, it would be wrong to conclude at this point that the Smithian world is based on banning all human passion with the result of creating a bleak sociability fit for domesticated androids. Non-mediated passions, in particular primary physical passions, are certainly considered antisocial. Of course, the 'interests' stemming from the sympathetic sentiments are more apt to guarantee communication, exchange and social cohesion (see section 2.2, 'The Economic Passion', for an in-depth discussion of the link between interests and sentiments). And yet, the passions survive. Without primary passions, there can be no secondary passions. With Adam Smith, the passions are neither denied their existence, nor are they simply suppressed. They are instead transformed, adapted and displaced into the economic sphere in order to allow social life to develop. One should not forget that the control of the passions only results from the strongest of them all: the desire 'to be beloved', which remains for Adam Smith the motor of the process of social construction.

The social function of wealth

In *The Theory of Moral Sentiments*, the principal objective of mankind is thus to be loved and respected or, at the least, not to be despised. The great paradox of Adam Smith's work, which constitutes a major obstacle to its full understanding, is that this eminently social motivation of being loved and accepted is at the origin of an economic self-interest that critics often consider as anti-social. We have already shown earlier that the control, moderation and transformation of the passions results in broadly shared and accepted sentiments, perceptions and values. From the assemblage of such shared values stems the *social function of wealth*, which assumes a key role in Adam Smith's vision of the working of a harmonious society.

In numerous passages of *The Theory of Moral Sentiments*, Smith stresses that the true value of wealth, whose accumulation is of course the aim of economic self-interest, does *not* reside in the comfort, physical well-being or security it can provide. This attitude occasionally includes the open disdain – at first degree – of economic well-being and wealth. One example is the following quotation, which will also play a role below in connection with the discussion of the invisible hand (see section 4.1):

> In ease of body and peace of mind, all the different ranks of life are nearly upon a level, and the beggar, who suns himself by the side of the highway, possesses that security which kings are fighting for.
>
> (Smith 1759 (IV.1.10): 216)

At second degree, however, economic wealth has tremendous value. This value is inherent in the respect, esteem, and appreciation it procures its owner in the eyes of his peers.

> Nothing is so mortifying as to be obliged to expose our distress to the view of the public, and to feel, that though our situation is open to the eyes of all mankind, no mortal conceives for us, the half of what we suffer. Nay, it is chiefly from this regard to the sentiments of mankind, that we pursue riches and avoid poverty … What is the end of avarice and ambition, of the pursuit of wealth, of power and pre-eminence? Is it to supply the necessities of nature? The wages of the meanest labourer can supply them … From whence then arises that emulation which runs through all the different ranks of men, and what are the advantages which we propose by that great purpose of human life which we call bettering our condition? To be observed, to be attended to, to be taken notice of with sympathy, complacency, and approbation, are all the advantages which we can propose to derive from it.
>
> (Smith 1759 (I.III.2.1): 61)

The word 'emulation', which refers to both 'competition' and 'mimesis', assumes a special significance in this context. Accumulating wealth is not only a movement of social differentiation but also of social mimesis. A rich man engages in the process of social emulation precisely in the same manner as his less fortunate peers, only that quantitatively he advances further. Of all the positive attributes of a man, material wealth is the one most easily perceptible and comprehensible, whose experience can be most easily shared. Since it consists entirely of exchangeable goods whose value is evident for all, material wealth becomes the ultimate *social* quality of the Smithian individual.

In acquiring wealth, men do not seek comfort or physical satisfaction but the emotional convergence, the sympathy, which arise from the shared understanding concerning the value of their wealth. A rich man receives satisfaction from his wealth only when experiencing the sympathy his wealth is able to generate. Given that it is easy to sympathise with him, the social appreciation of his wealth as 'valuable' is transferred through metonymic extension to its owner. With Adam Smith, *the principal use value of a good is its exchange value.* To its owner, an economic good is worth precisely what it is worth in the eyes of others, not more, not less.

A frequent misunderstanding maintains that pursuing individual wealth is an act of selfish nonconformity that defies shared social values.

Quite the opposite applies in Adam Smith's world. Consenting to socially shared perceptions of what is desirable as established by the sympathy mechanism, the Smithian individual joins the race for profits and thus becomes a useful member of the social order. It is thus logical that in Smith's work the pursuit of self-interest always demands the unconditional observance of the rules of the game. Disregarding these rules would eliminate any progress towards greater social esteem, which remains the essential motivation behind the pursuit of economic self-interest:

> In the race for wealth, and honours, and preferments, he [the individual] may run as hard as he can, and strain every nerve and every muscle, in order to outstrip all his competitors. But if he should justle, or throw down any of them the indulgence of the spectators is entirely at an end. It is a violation of fair play, which they cannot admit of.
>
> (Smith 1759 (II.II.2.1): 97)

Observing that the principal use value of an economic good consists in its exchange value, does not at all imply minimising the clear distinction that Smith draws between the two categories, for example, in the following well-known passage of *The Wealth of Nations*:

> The word VALUE, it is to be observed, has two different meanings, and sometimes expresses the utility of some particular object, and sometimes the power of purchasing other goods which the possession of that object conveys. The one may be called "value in use"; the other, "value in exchange".
>
> (Smith 1776 (I.I.4): 32)

It is useful, however, to consider the origins of this distinction and the relative importance of the two categories for economic reasoning. Also in *The Theory of Moral Sentiments* there exists a clear notion of use value, distinct from exchange value. This use value is always connected either to notions of physical well-being ('ease of body', 'conveniences to the body') or to notions of security and confidence ('tranquillity of mind', 'peace of mind', 'security' (all in Smith 1759 (IV.II.8–10): 212–16). Doubtless, these use values are in the eyes of the author of *Theory of Moral Sentiments* the true values, to which an enlightened man should aspire. With regard to wealth, however, Smith frequently points out how small the difference is that material wealth can make to the enjoyment of these authentic use values of bodily comfort and peace of mind.

In contrast, Adam Smith describes a number of particular objects that he considers to have great use value inasmuch they provide particular physical pleasures but little exchange value. Thus presenting a 'tooth-pick', an 'ear-picker' and a 'machine for cutting the nails', Smith underlines that these goods are very unlikely to elicit the envy of others, which means that despite their great usefulness they will be of little value. Once more, the economic value of a good is exclusively determined by its ability to generate the envy or appreciation of one's peers. Alone on an island, he continues, a man would most certainly prefer these so useful instruments 'even to a palace' (Smith 1759 (IV.1.10): 212–13).[3]

However, when living in society rather than alone on an island, things are different. In society, the social appreciation of material wealth and the exchangeable goods, to which it confers access, will dominate the esteem for true individual use values. Social, not private, estimation thus determines a good's value. The aesthetic appreciations of a good's *imagined* use has priority over the appreciation of its *actual* use. That the point is important is shown by the fact that Adam Smith claims, with uncharacteristic pride, to be the first to have noticed the gap between the socially perceived utility of a good and its true underlying use value:

> ... that the exact adjustment of the means of attaining any conveniency or pleasure, should frequently be more regarded, than the very conveniency or pleasure, in the attainment of which their whole merit would seem to consist, has not, so far as I know, been yet taken notice of by anybody.
>
> (Smith 1759 (IV.2.3): 210)

The reason for the divergence between the positive view of material wealth and its associated exchange value on the one hand and the relative disregard of use value on the other is, of course, once more that wealth procures the sympathetic identification of onlookers with the owner of the wealth. The 'concord' of sentiments and the social esteem that comes with it are the primary benefits the owner obtains from his wealth. In this process, the economically relevant utility of an object is captured by the look, the appearance, the suggestion and not by actual use or consumption. This holds both for the owner *and* for those who observe him. The ensuing convergence of sentiments concerning the value of a good through the sympathy mechanism establishes exchange value. This exchange value, however, is related to a virtual, fantasised use value that results from a shared aesthetic perception and which dominates any alternative value that could result from concrete individual usage:

> … the utility of any object … pleases the master by perpetually suggesting to him the pleasure or conveniency which it is fitted to promote. Every time he looks at it, he is put in mind of this pleasure … The spectator enters by sympathy into the sentiments of the master … .
>
> (Smith 1759 (IV.1.2): 209)

However, this process works both ways. Men prefer goods that are susceptible to generate sympathy, that is, goods that advertise their function in a particular visible manner rather than actually performing it.[4] Once sympathy is generated, the exchange value (in conjunction with an aesthetic, virtual use value) it establishes completely overrides any consideration of use value. This goes so far that for the man who lives in society the views of others are more important than his own perceptions. The fact that this derived use value is worthless in the eyes of the philosopher does not diminish its practical importance in daily life.

> If he is to live in society, indeed, there can be no comparison, because in this, as in all other cases, we constantly pay more regards to the sentiments of the spectator, than to those of the person principally concerned, and consider rather how this situation will appear to other people, than how it will appear to himself.
>
> (Smith 1759 (IV.2.8): 213)

The assimilation of a virtual use value and exchange value in the sympathy mechanisms and the de facto exclusion of true individual use value from social discourse are key steps in the foundation of economic rationality. Any notion of 'rationality' depends on a generally agreed metric against which behaviour can be assessed. The sympathy mechanism establishes 'wealth', the ability to acquire goods capable of generating sympathy, as the ultimate metric. The vital need to feel accepted by one's peers compels everybody to adopt this widely accepted, easily measurable and comprehensible metric. In a next step, everybody will try to advance as far as possible in the same direction. Henceforth, maximising individual wealth is identical with engaging in rational behaviour.

The *homo œconomicus* is an intensely social animal. His egoism and his pursuit of self-interest do not aim at wealth maximisation as an autonomous objective and a source of solipsistic pleasure. Instead, wealth is a means to acquire social recognition. The desire to maximise wealth (the pursuit of self-interest) is consubstantial to the desire of experiencing the convergence of sentiments in the sympathy mechanism. In a slightly provocative manner one could render the relationship that Smith develops here with the words 'wealth is love'. Due to the social function of wealth and due to the homogenisation of preferences via the sympathy mechanism, the *homo œconomicus* of microeconomic manuals ('rational' and 'individualist') can construct itself on the basis of a Smithian individual consumed by his desire for love, esteem and the respect of his peers. Utility maximisation in terms of goods with a socially recognised exchange value is thus just the formal expression of the unquenchable longing for social recognition.[5]

The satisfaction and the pleasure provided by such social recognition are sufficiently strong to motivate the search for wealth and fortune. This in return implies espousing the cardinal virtue which facilitates social recognition both directly and indirectly. This virtue is prudence. Prudence in the sense of restraint or circumspection helps both to acquire and protect social status directly, since it will censure any displays of extreme emotions, and indirectly, since it helps to acquire wealth. There is thus a double motivation to adopt it:

> The desire of becoming the proper objects of this respect, of deserving and obtaining the credit and rank among our equals, is, perhaps, the strongest of all our desires, and our anxiety to obtain the advantages of fortune is accordingly much more excited and irritated by this desire, than by that of supplying all the necessities and conveniencies of the body, which are always very easily supplied … The care of the health, of the fortune, of the rank and reputation of the individual, the objects upon which his comfort and happiness in this life are supposed principally to depend, is considered as the proper business of that virtue which is commonly called Prudence.
>
> (Smith 1759 (VI.I.3–4): 249)[6]

Already in an earlier chapter Smith had underlined the positive role prudence plays in connection with industry with regard to wealth acquisition:

> What is the reward most proper for encouraging industry, prudence, and circumspection? Success in every sort of business.
>
> (Smith 1759 (III.5.8): 193)

Thus a virtuous circle comes about, in which pursuing social virtues such as prudence is doubly rewarding. They facilitate the direct establishment of sympathy and the resulting commercial success makes the person concerned even more attractive.

The virtue of prudence strengthens the role of sympathy as the principal process for structuring social behaviour. Observing the orders of the impartial spectator, following virtues such as generosity and justice, cannot guarantee on its own the functioning of social life despite its noble pre-eminence (see Chapter 3 'The vertical world of the impartial spectator'). From the frosty heights of these aristocratic virtues, man must yet climb down again to the placid plains of sympathy. The moderation of the passions and the acquisition of wealth remain the safest means for establishing mutual sympathy, which alone permits experiencing that vital feeling 'to be beloved'.

2.2 Codification and the reduction of transaction costs: from sympathy to the market

The formation of preferences through auto-referential feedback loops

The sympathy mechanism is essential in Adam Smith's work. Its role can hardly be overestimated, even if it is in competition with that second structuring principle, which is the impartial spectator. From this competition it emerges triumphantly as far as the direct organisation of social life is concerned, for which it will constitute the essential reference framework. It remains the great paradox of the Smithian world, however, that the legitimacy of the victorious framework depends on its overall capability to satisfy the objectives of the defeated principle: general welfare and the 'propagation of the species' (see Chapter 4 'The paradoxical synthesis'). And yet, from a microeconomic point of view, that is, a perspective concerned with the individual economic agent, the sympathy mechanism becomes for Smith the only basis for the construction of society in general, and for market society in particular. We will see that the economic deliberations, which are the main reason why we remain interested today in Adam Smith's work and person, are the logical and necessary consequences of the sympathy mechanism.

The preceding section presented in a general fashion the world created by the sympathy mechanism as a world craving for social recognition through the medium of material wealth. The term 'wealth' designated in this context the sum of the socially recognised values a man possesses in the eyes of his peers. This section will explore in more detail the nature and informational structure of the values that compose this wealth. Of course, this will not aim primarily at identifying this or that specific commodity. The essential quality of the values susceptible to play a role in the sympathy mechanism is that they are based on an interpersonal agreement, which is, in principle, perfectly general as long as the 'goods' in question satisfy certain informational criteria.

It is, in fact, perfectly possible to determine the informational and communicational structure of the values which are capable of generating sympathy. Such an analysis begins with the work of Jean-Pierre Dupuy on the feedback loops created by the sympathy mechanism. In a next step it is possible to show the consequences of these feedback loops for the establishment of a market economy. Examples stemming from *The Wealth of Nations* show how the informational structure elaborated in *The Theory of Moral Sentiments* is transferred without modification into the founding work of modern economics. This section will thus concentrate on this link between *The Theory of Moral Sentiments* and *The Wealth of Nations.*

In terms of an analytic representation of the sympathy mechanism, Jean-Pierre Dupuy was the first of Adam Smith's critics to characterise the sympathy mechanism correctly as a form of auto-organisation on the basis of auto-reflective signals sent by different agents. The reciprocal mimesis of participating individuals is motivated by the desire to be loved and the pleasure that is obtained from having 'sympathetic' sentiments coincide. Dupuy notes that 'sympathy thus resembles a principle of contagion or imitation' (Dupuy 1988: 79, our translation). Dupuy's decisive contribution was to understand this reciprocal mimesis as a recursive or auto-reflective system with all the consequences this implies. 'The key is found in the notion of a recursive system, which implies codetermination between all parties' (Dupuy 1988: 75, our translation).

This recursive nature of the communication loops, with no link to any external references, also implies the essentially arbitrary character of the objects serving to attract and fix the sentiments that are standardised in this manner. Second, it explains the great stability of these 'strange attractors' once the self-reinforcing feedback loops have developed around it. The fact that Adam Smith describes society as a 'mirror', a paradigmatic example of a recursive system between an observer and his image, takes on added importance in this context. It is well known from chaos theory, for instance, that such recursive systems display at the same time an intrinsic indeterminateness of the final outcome *ex ante* and a very high degree of convergence towards this outcome once it has been established.

Valuable goods become 'strange attractors' justified by no other quality than their ability to serve as a point of convergence for the feelings of different individuals. It is of little interest to identify the specific objects and their representations, which are reflected and re-reflected in the visual perceptions of all and sundry. Essentially any object may serve to set in motion the vertiginous vortex of self-referential communication. 'The logical form at work is that of a self-referential loop which links the subject to itself by way of societal intermediation' (Dupuy 1988: 80, our translation). Remember that the sympathy mechanism is essential for steadying the sense of self of the Smithian individual, who finds stability only when he observes the coincidence of his feelings with those of others.

At the end of this process the 'sentiments' develop as the inferences of the different original passions transformed by the craving for social acceptance. In the course of this interpersonal, social interaction, only the shared and communicable part of the passions survives. This acceptable part of the passions can be signified and expressed in words, pictures or, more generally speaking, signifiers, which become binding references also for newcomers, who have only just joined the process.[7] The shared inferences thus temporarily acquire a certain stability or inertia. This inertia ensures that the shared sentiments, or the economic values once these sentiments attach themselves to tradable goods, are at the same time arbitrary *ex ante* and perfectly determined *ex post*. In the process, the self-referential feedback loops find their 'strange attractors' in precise objects. Smith mentions in this context, for instance, a palace, a beautiful garden or liveried servants (Smith 1759 (IV.1.8): 212). This link between a mental image associated with a certain notion of value on the one hand and a well-defined physical object on the other will constitute the *code* of economic values (see below). The values and objects, as well as the code they constitute, can be changed, but only in a discontinuous manner, once a new auto-reflective process comes to closure.

Without the impartial spectator whose presence, as we shall see, allows a more open form of value formation 'sympathy turns society into a self-referentially closed system with a circular causality between all participating parties' (Dupuy 1988: 84, our translation). For Dupuy this implies the need to abandon methodological individualism as the default methodology in economic theory. By characterising the sympathy mechanism as a process of creating a closed self-referential system of values, Jean-Pierre Dupuy made a breakthrough in understanding the process of preference formation in Adam Smith's work. Yet his conclusion to abandon the individual at the centre of Smith's work once more unduly simplifies the latter's vision of society. It substitutes, in fact, 'Smith, the eulogist of individualism' with 'Smith, the propagator of the social formation of values'. His conclusion, in fact, confuses the formation of values, which is indeed a social process, and the actions that are derived from them, which remain part of a strictly individual process.

The fertility of Adam Smith's work resides in the tension it is capable of sustaining. Once values are socially codified, the Smithian individual acts, in fact, as an entirely autonomous entity with *fixed* preferences. The *homo œconomicus* as individualist remains Smith's lasting creation but his individualism is formatted by social processes and imbued with a desire for social recognition. His choices are quantitatively autonomous and qualitatively determined by a process in which he participated but which he did not control. The coexistence of a complete local autonomy of individual actions and the firm, collective predetermination of the dimensions in which this autonomy can manifest itself is, since Adam Smith, the defining characteristic of economic science. Once the sympathy mechanism has been concluded, an individual no longer has a choice concerning the price-quantity plane in which he wants to operate, neither is there a continuum of such planes. He has, however, the freedom to choose his precise point in any of the planes at his disposal in function of the specific position he has assumed as a result of the sympathy mechanism.

The tension between the social formation of preferences and individual wealth maximisation naturally poses the question whether the two processes take place in parallel or in sequence. The answer is clear. In a first step, the sympathy mechanism codifies the preferences of the economic agents in a definite manner. Only once this process is concluded, will they pursue their 'self-interest' and the maximisation of their utility on the basis of these preferences, which will no longer change during the process. Smith's work is thus characterised by a methodological individualism preceded by the social formation of preferences. The two processes are strictly distinct and no economic action takes place before the codification of preferences. Adam Smith's description of the origins of the sympathy mechanism in the courtyards of primary school underlines the sequential order of preference formation and action based on these preferences. The sequence of his two principal works, *The Theory of Moral Sentiments* and *The Wealth of Nations* respects the same order. The relationship between the two books is defined by the relationship between preference formation and resulting economic action, each book concentrating on one single item. The Adam Smith Problem vanishes once one grasps the complementary but strictly distinct nature of social preference formation and individual economic action.

While the system of preferences resulting from the sympathy mechanism is perfectly determined from an *ex post* point of view for the participants, it is perfectly arbitrary from an *ex ante* point of view, before the process of reciprocal mimesis has started. Such a system has a number of specifically economic implications. If the values defined by these preferences are thus arbitrary for an observer outside the system, that is, an observer who is not partaking in the sympathy mechanism, there can be no objective or absolute notion of value in *The Theory of Moral Sentiments*. The same holds for *The Wealth of Nations*. The obvious objection to this statement is, of course, that Smith, as the founding father of the labour theory of value, has instituted labour as a source of objective value. The phrase that 'Labour … is the real measure of the exchangeable value of all commodities' (Smith 1776 (I.I.5): 34) is part of the basic stock of knowledge in the history of economic thought. However, this sentence must be understood in the context of the double distinction between 'commanded labour' and 'incorporated labour' on the one hand and between the measure of value and the formation of value on the other. We will see that a *measure* of value based on the notion of commanded labour is perfectly compatible with a *formation* of value through the self-referential feedback loops of the sympathy mechanism.

The distinction between the measure and the formation of value is recalled emphatically by Françoise Dubœuf in her article 'Travail commandé, travail incorporé, de Smith à Ricardo: analyse d'un malentendu' ('Commanded Labour and Incorporated Labour from Smith to Ricardo: the Analysis of a Misunderstanding'). In a first step, certain physical objects are imbued with value through inter-subjective processes but without that this value is being measured. In a second step, the units of labour that one can obtain in exchange for these objects provide the quantitative measure of their value. For Adam Smith, it is thus 'commanded labour', which provides a good's measure of value although it does not intervene in its formation, which remains due to the interpersonal sympathy mechanism.[8] And the phrase cited above should not be read without taking into account the surrounding paragraph:

> The value of any commodity … to the person who possesses it, and who means not to use or consume it himself, but to

> exchange it for other commodities, is equal to the quantity of labour which it enables him to purchase or command ... Labour was the first price, the original purchase-money that was paid for all things.
>
> (Smith 1776 (I.I.5): 34–35)

Labour thus is the price and the purchase-money of all goods. Labour is a medium of exchange, an intermediary, before being also a factor of production, whose contribution to output, however, provides scant information about the value of the final product. Labour is never the *source* of value for Adam Smith. Its establishment as the measure of value operates precisely not by way of its productivity but by way of its disutility, the displeasure and pain that it causes. Labour is measureable toil. Value is established otherwise. It is thus logical that the rate at which labour is exchanged for goods is arbitrary and not defined by any intrinsic link, even though the effort, the disutility, for each unit of labour is fixed:

> Equal quantities of labour, at all times and places, may be said to be of equal value to the labourer. ... he must always lay down the same portion of his ease, his liberty, and his happiness. The price which he pays must always be the same, whatever may be the quantity of goods which he receives in return for it.
>
> (Smith 1776 (I.I.5): 37)[9]

Françoise Dubœuf underlines that, in the *Wealth of Nations*, Adam Smith was primarily interested in the measure and not the formation of value. (We would add that he solved the problem of the formation of value in *The Theory of Moral Sentiments.*) It was only with David Ricardo's production-oriented approach centred on incorporated labour and his highly personal adaptation of Smith that economic science took an 'objectivist' turn. David Ricardo would probably agree with such a distinction. In fact, he had fully understood that Smith defended the independence of value formation from considerations of incorporated labour and criticizes him sharply in the chapter 'On Value' in his *Principles*:

> It cannot then be correct, to say with Adam Smith, 'that as labour may sometimes *purchase* a greater, and sometimes a smaller quantity of goods, it is their value which varies, not that of the labour which purchases them.
>
> (Ricardo 1821: 12)

With Ricardo, the measure of a good's value and the measure of the labour that is incorporated in it can only vary in parallel given that they maintain an intrinsic link, the amount of labour determining the good's value. With Smith, instead, this link between value and labour is transitory and conventional. Determined by the sympathy mechanism, the values in Smith's world are neither absolute, nor fixed in the long term, even if they enjoy considerable stability in the short term. The values thus established also do not carry any traces of a personal or collective history; they exist in a timeless present until they are replaced by other values that meanwhile work better as focal points for the collective convergence of sentiments. Labour just *measures* these conventional values, which are compelling only for the participating individuals but arbitrary from an external point of view.

Even more so, labour is of a fundamentally different quality from the exchangeable economic goods it measures, as for Adam Smith it remains outside the inter-subjective game of sympathy. And precisely because labour remains outside the mechanism of mutual mimesis between equals, it can assume its role as an independent and inalterable measure of value. Smith highlights the links of labour both to the notion of power ('Wealth … is power … a certain command over all the labour … which is then in the market' (WN, I.I.5): 35)) and to the physical sphere as labour is 'the toil of our own body' (ibid.). Contrary to the mirror image of the 'other', which belongs to the realm of imagination and imbues certain goods with the magical quality of making its owner more attractive, labour belongs to the sphere of real, physical sensations. Labour belongs to the sphere of the inalienable body, the primary, non-communicable passions and ultimately to the realm of the impartial spectator. It remains outside the mechanism of sociable auto-reflexivity and thus can assume its role as a credible yardstick of value (see also section 3.2 'Passions and interests or ethics and morality').

From image to action: the codification of the Smithian world

The sympathy mechanism thus creates fixed and discrete values, which are semantically closed. Notions such as 'beautiful house', 'garden' or 'liveried servant' are cleansed of all individual sensory experience that may arise from personal use. Instead, they are firmly linked to universally shared mental images. In other words, these notions are now firmly *codified*. This has important implications for the structure of economic behaviour *sensu stricto*. In order to fully understand the link between codification, the pursuit of self-interest and both economic theory and practice, it is useful to first define the concept of codification with precision.

An initial, simple definition of codification is provided by Dominique Foray in the context of knowledge management. Knowledge in this context, however, is a broad concept including any conscious inner representation of an object or notion transmitted by the five senses:

> The codification of knowledge is the process of converting knowledge into a message, which then can be manipulated as information … codified knowledge approaches the qualities of a commodity.
>
> (Foray 2000: 48, our translation)

This definition is largely equivalent to the one provided by Kenneth Arrow, which has the added advantage of referring immediately to the division of labour, a link we shall explore further below:

> To cooperate and to take advantage of the division of labor, there must be an exchange of information in one way or another. Let us draw upon … information theory … [which considers that] communication is a costly operation … Roughly speaking, you want to phrase the messages that occur most frequently in as short a way as possible … Concepts used repeatedly are given short technical names, so that a couple of words convey a whole thought … This is an illustration of the process that is sometimes called "encoding".
>
> (Arrow 1979: 161)

These first general definitions provide an initial intuition for what 'codification' might be. However, in order for it to be fully satisfying one would need to develop the concepts of a 'message', 'information' or 'communication'. Instead of embarking on the perilous task of a definition of definitions, we will present a short summary of the work on this subject by the historian of thought and semiotician Umberto Eco, an approach that is both rigorous and easily accessible. His analytical framework will then allow us to determine the structure of Smith's procedure with precision.

According to Eco, codification establishes the rules that link two or more structured systems (Eco 1984: 49–50). The set of these rules is called a code. Semiotics traditionally distinguishes three structured systems: a syntactic system, a semantic system and a system of actions. Each system possesses a structure that precisely defines the position of each of its elements. It is not necessary that these structures have 'meaning'.

Meaning in fact is generated only through codification, that is, the linking of two or more structured systems with each other. This is precisely the function of a code, the set of rules linking two or more systems. Such meaning can, for instance, be created by linking a series of indicators to a series of states of nature with different implications for human well-being to which each one requires a different response. One may think of a thermometer indicating a patient's temperature, which allows deductions about his health and the medicine the physician will choose in response. Umberto Eco himself chooses the example of a hydropower dam, where lights of different colours (the syntactic system) indicate different water levels (the semantic system), each one of which requires the operator to open or close a specific valve (the system of actions).

In particular the syntactic system is on its own void of all meaning – flashing red lights may serve as decoration for an office party as much as an alarm to open the valves. Without a code that links it to a semantic system, an isolated syntactic system does not signify anything, even if its structure (number of lights, their frequency, brightness and colour) can be precisely identified. One may think of the letters of the alphabet of an unknown language and the different combinations one can generate with it. Only the metasystem composed of a syntactic and a semantic system – such as words which link combinations of letters to mental pictures and ideas – generates meaning. That is even the principal function of such a metasystem and of the code that defines its internal structure.

Such a code composed of a syntactic system, a semantic system and a system of responses exists also for the informational structure of the world that Adam Smith develops in *The Theory of Moral Sentiments* and *The Wealth of Nations* and which is precisely composed of these three subsystems. Going further, one can state that the organisation of human behaviour and its representations in terms of identifiable codes is the necessary and, more surprisingly, sufficient condition for economics to emerge as an independent theoretical enterprise with legitimate scientific aspirations.

The syntactic system in this context corresponds to the set of the goods and physical objects apt to be imbued with economic value. At this point, it is not important whether the good in question actually *has* value. But it does need to have the informational characteristics necessary to be able to serve as a focal point in the process of sympathetic convergence. It needs to be an *economic* good, a commodity, easy to define and communicate, understood by all. Smith's oft criticised attitude towards services is entirely logical from this point of view. He rejects services as devoid of economic meaning (and hence value), because they seem to elude the clear-cut determination of their position in the system of economic goods (see next section for a detailed discussion).

The semantic system corresponds to the different sentiments, feelings or values an individual may feel when owning or acquiring the economic goods that constitute the syntactic system. It is thus made up of notions such as 'attraction', 'appreciation', 'disdain', 'indifference' and so on. In economic terms, one is dealing with preferences. A third system is composed of the possible economic responses. It consists of actions such as 'buy', 'sell', 'invest', 'save', 'wait' and so on. Between these three subsystems two major drivers, the sympathy process and the peculiar self-interest that results from it, will define the links and correspondences, which in their totality create a very tight and complete code. The sympathy mechanism and economic self-interest thus have complementary functions and together structure Adam Smith's world.

The codification of the syntactic system (goods and objects) and the semantic system (preferences and emotional reactions) is ensured by the sympathy mechanism – this is the great theme of *the Theory of Moral Sentiments*. To be precise, sympathy has two distinct functions in this context. The primary function is indeed the systematic linking (codification) of the syntactic and the semantic system. The secondary function is the structuring of the semantic system itself, a task that in time precedes the codification proper. One might call this the segmentation of the continuum of the emotions. This is what happens when 'original passions' are transformed into 'secondary passions', to use Smith's expression, or socially acceptable, moral 'sentiments'. In *The Theory of Moral Sentiments*, all sentiments that can be communicated have been created or modified by the sympathy mechanism. The sympathy mechanism not only links economically relevant 'sentiments' to specific objects and thus establishes a code of valuable goods, but also establishes the semantic system of possible economic values itself.

Economic self-interest links this first metasystem, which contains all the economically relevant information, with the system of possible responses – this is the great theme of *The Wealth of Nations*. This also allows the precise formulation of the *Adam Smith Problem*. In fact, the two books are not ruled by the same underlying principle. The misunderstanding that has persisted for far too long, however, is that the two principles should therefore be alternative or even contradictory. Not at all. The first principle ruling human behaviour, the sympathy mechanism, is the necessary condition for the second. Self-interest could not accomplish its task of linking preferences with consistent economic actions without the completion of the preceding step by the sympathy mechanism. *The Theory of Moral Sentiments* realises the first step in the codification process by way of the sympathy mechanism. In the following, the economic values thus created become the implicit basis for *The Wealth of Nations.* The table below synthesises this interaction.

The first codification between objects and values, sentiments or preferences through the sympathy mechanism is exceedingly stable. The code thus established is in fact *closed*, the links between objects and their economic values are clear, comparable and recursive. In the technical language of semiotics, the world described in *The Wealth of Nations*, which is the outcome of the sympathy mechanism, is characterised by an 'iconic' form of signification. This means that the correspondence between the sign and the signified object is so strong that under certain conditions, the former may substitute itself for the latter.[10] One may recall in this context that for Smith the *imagined* use value of an object has precedence over its actual use value in the determination of market value. The sign and its socially determinated content dominate the individual reality it is supposed to signify.

An iconic signification is always established in a powerful and definitive manner. The link between the sign, its meaning and the action that it implies, is devoid of any ambiguity, openness or irony. For an observer inside the communication system under consideration, such an iconic signification thus appears at the same time as instantaneous and permanent. Iconic signs bear no trace of the process of their creation and are thus perceived as 'evident' and 'natural'.

An iconic sign cries out 'what you see is what you get'. In our context this means that the link between a physical object and its economic

Table 2.1 Codification of the Smithian Universe through Sympathy and Self-interest

Syntactic system	Goods and objects (house, garden, carriage…)		
Semantic system	Emotional reaction or preference: appreciation, disdain, indifference …)	In *TMS*, sympathy creates the code of *economic values*	In *WN*, self-interest creates the code of *economic actions*
System of actions	Response action (buy, sell, invest…)		

value is no longer an issue depending on, say, circumstance, personal use value or other related conditions. Once codified, the physical object and its value are no longer distinguished as separate entities.

This over-determination that results from the closure of the semantic set has made the very idea of iconic signification problematic for a number of commentators. Umberto Eco himself, for example, questioned whether completely decontextualised signification, and with it the notion of iconicity, is practically possible (see his 'Critica dell'iconismo' in Eco 1984: 257–84). The pertinence of the notion of iconicity, in this essay as elsewhere, relies thus on its capacity to indicate an informational boundary rather than an everyday experience. In our context, one may argue that the effort of the Smithian individual, pushed by his desire for social acceptance to codify his perceptions of economic value, always runs the risk of being perturbed by a residue of individual experience with concrete use value that is not entirely codifiable and communicable. The relationship with the impartial spectator would also tend to disturb the process of codification, a problem that is only resolved once he his excluded from direct interference in human affairs.

We have said before that involvement with the sympathy mechanism requires effort. The same holds for engaging in iconic signification. Umberto Eco, for instance, underlines the fact that an iconic code – to the extent that it can be identified as such – always depends on a preceding configuration of the perceptive experience itself:

> We can now talk of an *iconic code* as a system that ensures the correspondence between a system of graphic elements and perceptive or cultural units that have been codified, that is, the pertinent units of a semantic system that depends on a *prior codification of the perceptive experience itself*'.
>
> (Eco 1984: 274, our translation)

Of course, establishing such a codification of the perceptive experience by way of converging the experiences of two or more persons is exactly the *raison d'être* of the sympathy mechanism. These perceptions will ultimately deliver notions of the surrounding reality that are perfectly shared and thus 'evident'. In his desire for social recognition and affection and in order to break out of the mute prison of the passions, the Smithian individual will force himself to find attractive, unsightly or middling the goods which maximise the probability that his peers react the same way. This, however, precisely requires the prior codification of the perceptive experience itself.

The notion of iconicity thus applies perfectly to the form of communication outlined by Adam Smith. The informational structure that results from the sympathy mechanism does not leave the slightest margin for interpretation between the sign and its meaning. The Smithian individual, and later the economic agent, perceives the link between the sign, the mental image it produces and its real-world counterpart as natural, unbreakable and compelling. The very etymology of the word 'economy', composed from the Greek words *oikos* (household) and *nomos* (the law), provides an idea of the coercive nature of this conceptual codification. The fact that, from a point of view outside of the self-referential loops created by the sympathy mechanism, these perceptions are the result of largely arbitrary conventions, does not in the least diminish their role in structuring the economic environment (see below). On the contrary, precisely because the conventional values are arbitrary, they force the Smithian individual to abandon any link with alternative references (usually personal sensory experience or communication with the impartial spectator). He is consequently all the more condemned to cling to the shared references provided by the sympathy mechanism.

Of course, one should never confuse the particular informational structure that Adam Smith *describes* in the context of the sympathy mechanism with the informational structure the author *practices* himself in his works. Smith is a stylist and a rhetorician of the very first rank and his writings are the result of the careful management of an extreme tension. It also needs to be stressed that the communication of the Smithian individual with the impartial spectator belongs to the symbolic, rather than the iconic, type (see Chapter 3 'The Vertical World of the Impartial Spectator' for an in-depth discussion). Nevertheless, the iconic signification created by the sympathy mechanism constitutes the definitive informational basis for the individual economic behaviour analysed in *The Wealth of Nations*.

Once reliably established, the firm and definitive codification of concepts and values has profound economic implications due to the reduction of transaction costs that it implies. It is a necessary and sufficient requirement for commoditisation and a precondition for true economic reasoning and behaviour. In Smith's work, the reduction of transaction costs following the codification of economic objects and their valuable nature is the founding act of a market economy as well as the starting point for its coherent theoretical representation.

There exist multiple aspects of the link between economic behaviour and economic theory, where a truly iconic codification is the horizon towards which the system tends. One illustrative aspect is the well-known difficulty of economic science to integrate change and historical time, since this runs counter to the codification required from its concepts. Historical time introduces evolutionary change, complexity and nuance. This does not allow establishing definitive concepts. The very generality of economic representation implies its static nature. However, bringing the process of the formation of meaning to a close in order to establish concepts that are static implies discontinuities in the representation of a complex and changing reality.

The existence of such discontinuities is implicit in all codification. Cutting through the unstructured mass of sensory perceptions in order to establish communicable units is the very nature of signification. Dominique Foray expresses this with the words: ' … the task of codification is not only a task of transfer but also a work of creation which includes proceeding to new divisions and re-compositions of knowledge' (Foray 2000: 50, our translation). Due to its extremely static nature, it is typical of iconic signification that such discontinuities manifest themselves more quickly and in a more pronounced fashion than with other forms of signification.

The necessary adjustments to catch up with an eternally changing reality thus happen also in a discontinuous manner. It is an interesting quality of economic systems that these adjustments in themselves – as adjustments – can be highly codified. 'Fashion' is the purest example for such a process, since by definition it is devoid of any disturbing residue of use value. In order not to lose the vital nexus to shared perceptions, change in fashion takes place between well established opposites that serve as reference: short skirts – long skirts, relaxed style – formal style etc. Today, one can observe similar processes in the periodic improvements concerning technological performance, which have become by themselves themes of codification (a 'greener' car, a faster microcomputer, a mobile phone with more functionalities etc.). In such an iconic, or economic, universe, the need for untrammelled communication thus even structures innovation.

The whole issue of 'external effects' also elucidates the link between economics and codification. An externality is by definition a good whose impact on well-being is recognised but which remains excluded from economic discourse and action since it lacks the essential quality of economic good: to be fully codified and communicable (Keppler 1998a). The residual category of externalities is in fact identical with the category of un-codified goods.

On occasion, the economic implications of codification are even recognised by standard economic theory. For instance, every economic codification that succeeds in creating a universally established standard creates the phenomenon of 'winner-takes-all', well-known in the theory of networks. A good example is the software industry, whose business is, of course only that – creating codes. Every successful codification is thus 'conservative' in nature: any newly introduced product needs to promise more than marginal improvements in order to be accepted. An existing and widely adopted software package will always have advantages over a newer one, which imposes penalties on its users in terms of technical and practical 'connectivity', industry shorthand for its inability to create widely shared perceptions of its value.

With Adam Smith, a similar conservatism can be indentified in his insistence on 'real' values. In the world he outlines, a good's principal value resides in its quality of being socially recognisable. A good whose characteristics are difficult to communicate loses the essential part of its value. A solid value associated with well-established preferences will always win out over a new product whose social acceptability still needs to be proven (see below the disparaging remarks that Smith reserves for services 'which do not *fix* themselves').

Before taking a closer look at the iconic world of *The Wealth of Nations*, it is useful to summarise the line of reasoning developed so far. In Smith's work, a first codification between objects and their social value through the sympathy mechanism creates economic goods. A second codification, driven by a socially formatted self-interest establishes the links between these economic goods and the set of economic actions. The structuring force of self-interest is indeed the central theme of *The Wealth of Nations* and its power to codify the links between goods and actions sets the foundation for the enterprise to establish economics as a scientific discipline. And yet in informational terms, outlining this process is relatively straightforward given that the set of economic actions is constituted by a limited number of well-defined actions. Once *The Theory of Moral Sentiments* has shown how the code of economic *values* is established, Adam Smith can deduce the consequences in a nearly exhaustive manner and present all the permutations of the code of economic actions in *The Wealth of Nations.*

The iconic world of The Wealth of Nations

Market society is the necessary consequence of the sympathy mechanism which provides all the conditions that are necessary for its existence. This is what is shown by *The Wealth of Nations.* On a psychological level, the desire to exchange, 'the propensity to truck and barter' is the extension of the wish to create that pleasant coincidence of two mental universes which remains the objective of the sympathy mechanism.[11] The very act of exchanging and the division of labour, which is of course a precondition for all exchange, thus become the tangible proof for the establishment of mutual sympathy. All value in *The Wealth of Nations* is thus always and everywhere exchangeable value.

But the sympathy mechanism not only provides the impetus for the creation of a society of merchants seeking the pleasures of sociability through market-based trading. The sympathy mechanism also creates on a more formal level all the necessary conditions for the development of such a society of merchants. The codification of all economic values through the sympathy mechanism implies inevitably the reduction of transaction costs, the division of labour, constant returns to scale and competitive markets. The role of transaction costs is, of course, crucial in this context. In the iconic universe of *The Wealth of Nations* each value is definitively codified, immediately recognisable for all and its transfer during an exchange is thus free of transaction costs.

Adam Smith's genius resides in the fact that this perfectly codified universe does not jump fully armed out of its creator's head by hypothesis but is patiently constructed throughout the texts. In a first step, *The Theory of Moral Sentiments* elaborates the anthropological and psychological foundations of a society, which vitally depends on unequivocal communication. In a second step, *The Wealth of Nations* develops the panorama of a society without informational transaction costs. Beyond that, the book also systematically deconstructs each and every instance that might constitute a threat for the stable codification of economic values and that could thus reintroduce informational transaction costs in exchange.

Adam Smith is far too astute an observer of reality to situate himself *a priori* in a universe without transaction costs. Such a universe, however, remains the horizon of his argument. The world of *The Wealth of Nations* is not a world without transaction costs but a world in which all transaction costs can, in principle, be objectified, codified and monetised. Smith himself dedicates himself to this work of codification. This codification transforms transaction costs, which otherwise would constitute a source of inefficiency and monopoly, into factors of production that no longer pose any threat for competitive markets. The easiest way to imagine such a process is to think of transport costs, which can be thought of either as a transaction cost or as a codified and monetised input to the provision of a specific good at a specific time and thus can be very well accommodated in a complete set of competitive markets. The example provided by Adam Smith concerns the storage costs for precious metals, which would be, in principle, a transaction cost. However, through careful codification it is possible to value it precisely as a useful service in its own right:

> What is thus paid for the keeping of the deposit may be considered a sort of warehouse rent; and why this warehouse rent should be so much dearer for gold than for silver several different reasons have been assigned. The fineness of gold, it has been said, is more difficult to be ascertained than that of silver. Frauds are more easily practised, and occasion a greater loss in the more precious metal.
>
> (Smith 1776 (I.IV.3.1): 506)

Following this operation of codification, we are no longer facing an imperfect banking sector with transaction costs, but two competitive industries: the banking sector and a 'security industry' which provides storage and verification services for precious metals for the banks.

With the codification of economic values and the reduction of transaction costs the sympathy mechanism lays the basis for the division of labour. In this process, one can distinguish two separate operations. On the one hand, codification reduces transaction costs by creating perfectly defined exchangeable objects; on the other hand transaction costs such as transport costs are in themselves codified and thus transformed into monetised services. Beyond classic transaction costs, Smith seeks to neutralise systematically every instance which might introduce uncertainty about the value of a good and thus weaken its codification. This includes the sort of issue today referred to as an 'agency problem'. The question is anything but anodyne. General economic welfare can only be obtained in a semantically closed world. The invisible hand cannot function in a system in which the formation of preferences is still inconclusive (see also section 4.1 '"Efficient causes" and "final causes": the working of the invisible hand'). In fact, the *formation* of preferences – as opposed to their transmission or application – always has a 'public', communicative element. The individual optimisation of private interests in an economic setting ensues only once this process of preference formation has been concluded.

In the following, we will show in seven different instances how Adam Smith systematically attacks all elements that might threaten the firm codification of his economic system. These instances are: speculation, conspicuous consumption, services, fiat money, joint stock companies, monopolies and public goods. Despite individual particularities, Smith's criticism serves each time to forcefully assert the iconic signification that prevails in a well-working market economy. In a final section, we will show that the absence of informational transaction costs due to this iconic signification will necessarily result in a system of competitive markets with constant returns on a scale functioning at the level of the individual firm, even if increasing returns are present at the level of the industry and the economy as a whole. The 'normal' state of affairs in *The Wealth of Nations* is characterised by the absence of any issues of information or signification. This does not mean that such issues have disappeared altogether, but they are clearly pointed out as deviant and can be addressed on a case by case basis.

The first case concerns Adam Smith's professed aversion to those who build their projects on uncertain beliefs or hopes rather than on solid knowledge. 'Prodigals and projectors' or 'speculators', as he calls them, destroy value with unsound schemes. They also happen to be the same people who engage in a consumption of sterile services, in particular in the form of employing domestic servants (Smith 1776 (I.I.10.1): 127, (I.II.3): 368, (I.10.1): 121 et (II.3): 358). Their conspicuous consumption, which one might have considered a motor for the invisible hand in the spirit of Mandeville, is also severely criticised:

> … the conduct of every prodigal, by feeding the idle with the bread of the industrious, tends not only to beggar himself, but to impoverish the nation.
>
> (Smith 1776 (I.II.3): 360)

Smith identifies these two traits – speculation and conspicuous consumption – in the same group of people. What vexes him are not so much the specific impacts of their actions, which remain quite vague, but the fact that they generate, use and distribute unreliable information about economic values and thus supposedly destroy private *and* social wealth. There are only two ways to bring such privately and socially devious behaviour into line, either codification by the law ('any positive law, by any trust-right or deed of mortmain') or preferably, through, self-interest. The passage is not only of interest in our discussion about the role of codification of economic values. It also shows in a particularly clear manner that the pursuit of 'self-interest' for Adam Smith means in no way indulging in personal impulses but implies engaging in the socially useful act of increasing one's capital.

Opposed to the conspicuous consumption of sterile services are the display and the staging of solid durable goods in *The Theory of*

Moral Sentiments, which is rightly highlighted by Daniel Diatkine (Diatkine 1991: 32). Displaying one's wealth in a manner that permits everyone to appreciate it is a necessary step of gaining social appreciation through wealth acquisition. Smith's criticism of conspicuous consumption instead addresses individual, aristocratic whims indifferent to the acquisition of lasting personal wealth. 'Gratuitous' consumption thus results from the insufficient control of a passionate and aggressive egotism that eludes the mechanisms of social reflexivity. The display of goods, which are identical to those owned or coveted by one's peers, instead supports that reflexivity. The same issue will be addressed a century later by Thorstein Veblen, a close follower of Smith concerning the link between consumption and social standing.

The third case concerns the already mentioned disdain that Adam Smith expresses repeatedly for services or 'unproductive labour'; the two terms are actually used interchangeably. This disdain is due to the mistrust he has for all economic goods not immediately verifiable in their physical concreteness:

> The labour of a menial servant … adds to the value of nothing … A man grows rich by employing a multitude of manufacturers: he grows poor by maintaining a multitude of menial servants … The labour of the menial service … does not fix or realize itself in any particular subject or vendible commodity.
>
> (Smith 1776 (I.II.3): 351)

To be durably *fixed* and realised or revealed in a concrete and tangible manner remains for Adam Smith a decisive criterion for the constitution of reliable economic value. The desire to be able to socially authenticate a good's value in each and every instance dominates here the economic logic of preference satisfaction. This is quite remarkable. Even Edwin Cannan, one of Adam Smith most staunchly loyal followers, editor of the important 1904 edition of *The Wealth of Nations*, cannot help himself to note in an editorial footnote that in principle one should count only the utility of a service. For Adam Smith, however, a real economic *good*, is tangible, long-lasting and durably codified.

In a fourth case, the establishment of the iconic world of *The Wealth of Nations*, in which all things are what they appear to be, implies the forceful rebuttal of fiduciary money and the monetary 'illusion' that goes with it. Smith is virtually obsessed with the distinction between real and nominal values. Labour as the *measure* of a good's real value is, of course, the ultimate standard of all value. The central importance of the notion of labour in this context is due to its role as the anchor of the semantic system of values and not, as David Ricardo would later maintain, due to its role as the source of all value. However, the value of labour is not directly observable – precisely because it is outside of the arbitrary system of values derived from mutual sympathy – and its observable indicator, the real wage as a function of the price of corn, is subject to short-term variations. In this situation, the price of gold or silver may serve as an approximate standard of value in the medium term. Given that gold and silver are physically tangible and their quantity and purity are verifiable with precision, they are hugely preferable to any kind of fiduciary money based on transitory conventions. Adam Smith's rejection comes with an added dose of poetical flourish:

> The commerce and industry of the country … cannot be altogether so secure, when they are thus … suspended upon the Dædalian wings of paper money, as when they travel about upon the solid ground of gold and silver.
>
> (Smith 1776 (I.II.2): 341)

Of course, Adam Smith is acutely aware that the value of gold and silver is also ultimately determined by conventions and says so in the text. However, these stable, time-honoured, and seemingly natural conventions are preferable to new and untested ones, which have the added blemish of self-consciously advertising themselves as conventions, an unforgiveable act of semantic aperture in a world striving towards iconic closure. The solid base of historical precedence thus wins out over the experimentations of bold monetary policy.

The fifth case concerns Smith's critical evocation of constellations of asymmetric information and incentives that today are referred to as principal-agent problems. By common consensus the passage in question is considered the first presentation of an agency problem in economic literature. Adam Smith develops his criticism of the unfortunate consequences of the divergence of interests between owners and managers in the context of his discussion of 'joint stock' or public companies. Dismissing the limited capacity of company directors to exert effective control as representatives of the owners he writes:

> The directors of such companies … being the managers rather of other people's money than of their own, it cannot well be expected that they should watch over it with the same anxious vigilance with which the partners in a private copartnery frequently watch

> over their own … Negligence and profusion, therefore, must always prevail, more or less, in the management of the affairs of such a company. It is upon this account that joint stock companies … have seldom been able to maintain the competition against private adventurers.
>
> (Smith 1776 (I.V.1.3.1): 264–65)

The development of modern capitalism based on elaborate risk-sharing and the peculiar division of labour inherent in public companies does not support Smith's anxieties. Public companies allow managing both uncertainty, by allowing investors to diversify their capital, and complexity, by outsourcing specific management tasks to highly competent specialists. Uncertainty and complexity, however, are unwelcome and to some extent unnecessary disturbances once Smith has designated a system with a firm codification of preferences and parameters as being socially optimal. Again, a fully and definitely codified, or iconic, world remains the horizon rather than the immediate reality of *The Wealth of Nations*. What is remarkable is rather the systematic manner in which Adam Smith investigates all sources of semantic indeterminacy and makes himself the advocate of their suppression. In this light, public companies only introduce an added layer of always fragile communication and thus contribute for Adam Smith to uncertainty and complexity rather than to their management.

A similar line of argument is pursued with even greater force in the sixth case. Progress towards an iconic economic world in *The Wealth of Nations* plays itself out decisively in Smith's relentless attacks against all forms of monopoly, but in particular against monopolies having received exclusive government privileges. Two examples may serve to give the flavour of the numerous, frequently quite violent, passages concerning monopoly:

> Such exclusive companies, therefore, are nuisances in every respect; always more or less inconvenient to the countries in which they are established, and destructive to those which have the misfortune to fall under their government.
>
> (Smith 1776 (II.IV.7): 158)

And:

> The violence and injustice of the rulers of mankind is an ancient evil, for which, I am afraid, the nature of human affairs can scarce admit of any remedy. But the mean rapacity, the monopolizing

> spirit of merchants and manufacturers, who neither are, nor ought to be, the rulers of mankind, though it cannot perhaps be corrected, may very easily be prevented from disturbing the tranquillity of any body but themselves.
>
> (Smith 1776 (I.IV.3.2): 519)

On this point, conventional wisdom has it right: Adam Smith is the unwavering champion of open, competitive markets. There exist several motivations for Adam Smith's famously hostile attitude towards monopoly. The one that interests us here is the fact that the existence of monopoly always implies a certain informational opening and the absence of explicit codification. The formal definition of a monopoly is the imperfect substitutability of one firm's output with that of another one. Such *product differentiation* however is the opposite of codification. Exercising a monopoly means owning a unique technology or product that cannot be easily copied by actual or potential rivals. Monopoly, product differentiation and absence of codification imply each other.

This relationship can also be formulated in terms of transaction costs. The term 'transaction cost' in itself is a catch-all category for a non-codified residual in economic exchange. If this residual was codifiable, it would become, in its turn, a tradable good. Harold Hotelling (1929) and Ronald Coase (1937 and 1988) have both shown the link between transaction costs and monopoly power, the first for markets for consumer goods and the second for factor markets. In both cases the result is unambiguous: transaction costs and monopoly power are two faces of the same coin. The opposite is also true: the absence of transaction cost implies the absence of monopoly power and perfect competition. If a consumer can switch from one good to another without loss of utility, no producer can fix his price above the cost of production. A world without transaction costs is a world without monopoly and vice versa.

In the world of Adam Smith, the absence of transaction costs is guaranteed by the codifying force of the sympathy mechanism. The codification of all 'goods' and their value implies the absence of informational transaction costs and thus the absence of all transaction costs and perfect competition. The reason is the following. If the exchange of information is costless then any aspect of an economic transaction can be codified and transformed into an economic good. A transaction cost is thus transformed into a valuable economic good or service (Keppler 1998a). This is precisely the approach chosen by Adam Smith where all non-informational transaction costs such as transport are immediately monetised. They thus acquire the status of factor of production and no longer constitute a barrier to competition. Codification creates commodities, in the sense of Gérard Debreu's definition that '... a commodity is a good or a service completely specified physically, temporally, and spatially' (Debreu 1959: 32).

In the iconic world of *The Wealth of Nations*, perfect competition is therefore the natural state of affairs. Permanent monopoly power here is always due to political and legal barriers to new entrants. Trade secrets can at best provide short-term transitory monopoly power. Monopoly is thus based on legal privileges and not on intrinsic features of the production function such as increasing returns.[12] In an economic world, systematically formatted by the sympathy mechanism, there can be no 'natural' or technical monopolies:

> The price of monopoly is upon every occasion the highest which can be got ... Such enhancements of the market price may last as long as the regulations of police which give occasion to them.
> (Smith 1776 (I.I.7): 69–70)

Adam Smith's criticism of monopoly logically extends to the provision of public goods through government beyond a bare minimum that consists of defence, the administration of justice and primary education. This constitutes the seventh and final case of the Smithian philippic against all instances that may threaten the firm codification of the economic system. His acerbic assessment of government action is well known:

> But though the profusion of government must, undoubtedly, have retarded the natural progress of England towards wealth and improvement, it has not been able to stop it.
> (Smith 1776 (I.II.3): 367)

Smith even rejects, or at least severely curtails, the government's role in instances where it is generally considered necessary such as in the provision of public infrastructure, for example, the construction of canals and highways (Smith 1776 (II.V.1.3.1): 247). The standard argument is that governments are needed to internalise the positive externalities such public infrastructure provides. In a society without informational transaction costs, however, this argument no longer holds. If all benefits and costs are perfectly codified, the market can fully internalise all externalities on its own.

Smith's disregard for government action, beyond the three items mentioned above, is the direct consequence of his vision of a society without informational transaction costs. Like monopoly, the case for government always reposes on some form of informational opening. The very notions of 'politics' and 'polis' recall that matters need to be discussed in public before, while and after action is taken. A public good is a good whose features are so complex that one cannot separate its allocation from an ongoing process of the formation and adjustment of preferences. The same holds for externalities. An external effect is always the result of the over- or underproduction of too complex a good, that is a good with too high a transaction cost to be internalised by the market (see Arrow 1970: 76f).

In the case of Adam Smith, the absence of corrective political action to address the shortcomings of a market economy is the necessary corollary of the absence of informational transaction costs. The regret that, for instance, Dermange formulates in this respect is misplaced. Adam Smith's abstinence is not the sign of incoherence or lack of imagination. He is the first to point out the negative side-effects of a market economy such as in the famous passages concerning the stultifying impacts of the division of labour in Book V of *The Wealth of Nations*. However, in an iconic world where things are what they seem for all to see, any government can only disturb the socially beneficial interaction of competitive markets.

Nevertheless, Smith is not pursuing a radical libertarian agenda for its own sake. A government reduced to its core functions is not only considered admissible but necessary. Its role in upholding the rule of law, protecting property rights and curbing violence is a pre-condition for a market society even in the iconic world of *The Wealth of Nations*. The subordination of the violent passions to the individual quest for wealth in order to allow the sympathy mechanism to function has not abolished them, but only temporarily moderated and displaced them. The task of government is thus to protect the resulting market society and its socially beneficial outcomes. Section 3.2 'The Economic Passion' will discuss in more detail the core functions of government, which, according to Adam Smith, are defence, justice and primary education. These prerogatives of the state owe nothing to the sympathy mechanism and the desire for social recognition but derive from the ethical commands of the impartial spectator. The fact that, in their turn, they enable the sympathy mechanism to function by creating the necessary preconditions, notably the absence of fear of physical violence and the ability to partake in social exchange, foreshadows the paradoxical synthesis that Adam Smith proposes to his readers and that is the theme of Chapter 4.

The division of labour, constant returns and equilibrium: economics as science

Adam Smith's refusal to admit economic monopoly in any possible form implies an absence of government intervention and 'free competition' as the basic hypothesis for the structure of markets in *The Wealth of Nations.* And 'free competition' here is very close indeed to the 'perfect competition' presented in microeconomic textbooks with free entry and a price that is equal to both marginal and average cost. In addition to the absence of transaction costs, which in itself, guarantees competition, the division of labour and the permanent externalisation of distinct economic operations will ensure that fixed costs will never grow beyond a certain size and that constant returns to scale will prevail. The natural result is a price equal to average costs, at least in the long-run:

> The natural price, or the price of free competition … is the lowest which can be taken, not upon every occasion indeed, but for any considerable time altogether … [It] is the lowest which the sellers can commonly afford to take, and at the same time continue their business.
>
> (Smith 1776 (I.I.7): 69)

Of course, the theory of monopolistic competition shows that price may also equal average costs with increasing returns and inelastic demand. Yet several factors indicate that Adam Smith worked on the basis of a general hypothesis of competitive markets, in which the individual firm has no influence on price or demand, as long as there are no legal or administrative barriers to entry.

On the face of it, an obvious counter-argument is that surely Adam Smith believed in increasing returns through capital accumulation in the long-run. While this is true, the existence of increasing returns at the level of the economy or the industry in a dynamic perspective is compatible with the existence of constant returns at the firm level. As Allyn A. Young shows in his brilliant demonstration of the link between scale effects and market size in 'Increasing Returns and Economic Progress' (1928), the division of labour will keep the growth of an individual enterprise in check by spawning new sub-enterprises able to perform certain tasks. This limits monopoly power and ensures constant returns to scale at the firm level, all the while maintaining the dynamism of increasing returns at the level of the economy. Each time that an enterprise grows beyond a certain size, production will be partially externalised.

Of course, this process is only possible with an extremely solid codification of all the economic processes involved and the reduction in transaction costs that it implies. Foray describes this link between codification and the division of labour it makes possible as follows: that only the 'aptitude to codify knowledge permits externalisation' (Foray 2000: 48f, our translation). All forms of externalisation based on the division of labour require a clear definition of the products or inputs exchanged (technical specifications, colour, quality, size etc.).

Codification is also crucial for any division of labour internal to the firm. Smith transforms the paradigmatic example of the pin factory into a model for the codification of production processes in order to explain the benefits of the division of labour. The broad and relatively vague concept of 'making pins' is replaced by a number of highly precise notions such as 'drawing the wire', 'straightening it', 'cutting it', 'pointing it', 'grinding it at the top', 'putting the head on', 'whitening the pin', 'putting the pins into paper'. Smith states that he can thus distinguish (codify) 'eighteen different operations'. In the light of the ongoing externalisation highlighted by Allyn A. Young, the following phrase is of particular interest:

> … in the way in which this business is now carried on, not only the whole work is a peculiar trade, but it is divided into a number of branches, of which the greater part are likewise peculiar trades.
>
> (Smith 1776 (I.I.1): 8)

A sub-task of the process of pin-making inside a single establishment can thus grow into a new industry ('trade'). With the kind of codification we have just witnessed, each process is perfectly defined and codified and thus replicable. Codification, as anyone who has ever worked on technical standards can testify, is not only a necessary and sufficient condition for the division of labour, it also generates competition in a very direct and immediate manner.

A second argument against the idea that Adam Smith pursued a vision of monopolistic competition is the fact that all the entrepreneurs mentioned in *The Wealth of Nations* are clearly typified as being part of a general trade – the butcher, the farmer, the baker, the blacksmith etc. – without the slightest hint at product differentiation. Their formative mode of action remains the *emulation* already encountered in *The Theory of Moral Sentiments*, that is, a form of mimetic competition. There is no product differentiation in Adam Smith. Product differentiation would imply that the notion of a specific economic good is no longer perfectly closed and codified. Codification eliminates product differentiation and the monopoly power that comes with it. The absence of product differentiation is equivalent to the absence of economic, as opposed to legal or political, monopoly. Allowing for minor divergences in the short run, perfect competition remains logically the normal industrial structure in *The Wealth of Nations* with all the consequences in terms of price formation and welfare effects that this implies.

One may want to reply that capital accumulation plays an important role in *The Wealth of Nations* as an engine of growth. Such capital accumulation could be interpreted, as was done later by David Ricardo and Karl Marx, as an increase in fixed costs, the size of the firm and its monopoly power. However, following Adam Smith, such capital accumulation is an industry- or even economy-wide phenomenon that will lower average costs for all and will not result in the domination of a single establishment. Such increasing returns to scale through *historical time* do not pose a threat for competition. Smith's vision of industrial organisation does indeed combine competition *and* increasing returns to scale, the latter albeit at the level of the industry and not at the level of the individual firm. It was Alfred Marshall who tried most persistently to translate this dynamic vision of competition into the new language of comparative statics, which created theoretical issues of its own.[13] These technical issues, however, do not affect the coexistence of constant returns at the firm-level with increasing returns at the industry-level in *The Wealth of Nations.*

The second approach to understanding the coexistence of capital accumulation through time with constant returns to scale and perfect competition is Allyn A. Young's vision of a firm constantly spinning off newly codified tasks to sub-contractors as already mentioned above. Explicitly putting himself into the historical continuity of Adam Smith, Young in effect describes a firm with increasing capital intensity that at a certain point auto-dissolves and proceeds to a new division of labour between its component parts. The increasing returns, which are so beneficial for economic progress, thus manifest themselves neither at the level of the firm, nor, strictly speaking, at the level of the industry. They manifest themselves instead at the level of the economy as a whole, where new industries allowing a more efficient division of labour are being created. In this process, capital accumulation, technical progress and institutional re-organisation obviously go hand in hand, never allowing a single firm to gain the upper hand. Again, like in the Marshallian vision provided above, albeit for slightly different reasons, capital accumulation and increasing returns through time, do not pose a threat to competition.

We can thus confirm that constant returns to scale at the level of the firm and perfect competition are two fundamental hypotheses of Adam Smith in *The Wealth of Nations.* This is ultimately the consequence of the system of communication he developed in *The Theory of Moral Sentiments* that implied the full codification of all economic values and the absence of informational transaction costs. This link between the absence of transaction costs and the absence of monopoly power is, of course, just the illustration of Coase's insight that in a world without transaction costs a firm's size tends towards zero and thus satisfies the condition of 'atomicity' demanded for the existence of perfectly competitive markets. Adam Smith's view of the economy – as long as government abstains from tampering with it – is indeed that of a world of small-scale shopkeepers.

Smith's attacks against monopolies and government, the ultimate monopoly, are in this perspective the result of a vision that demands that all value should be evident and amenable to iconic signification. Monopolies and government threaten the semantic closure of the system. When governments sponsor legal monopolies while making vague promises of positive externalities such as exporting civilisation to far-away colonies or the greatness of the nation, they are acting amorally in the full sense of the word. Such positive externalities are not part of the universally accepted values codified by the interpersonal sympathy mechanism. (For a distinction between social morality and individual ethics see section 3.2 'The economic passion'.) The final phrases of *The Wealth of Nations* constitute a poignant example in this connection. Smith's admonition to the British political leadership to satisfy itself with an external policy corresponding to the real stature of their country rejects any visions of national splendour and confirms that the responsibility of government lies in creating the conditions for the economic advancement of its citizens.

The Theory of Moral Sentiments remains the direct precursor of *The Wealth of Nations* in preparing the latter's underlying informational structure. This has two major implications. First, as we have seen above, it thus provides the necessary and sufficient condition for the omnipresence of competitive markets. However, just as important is that the informational closure of all economic notions, which is at the heart of the market society in *The Wealth of Nations,* is also the decisive step in setting up an economic science that can legitimately aspire to a status equivalent to that of the natural sciences. Codification permits not only abstraction and mathematical formulation. More importantly, the scientific character of economics is henceforth underwritten by the fact that it only studies highly codified exchange values, which are perfectly accepted by all and which hence assume an evident, even natural, air. In fact, only their generalised acceptance establishes them as economic values in the first place.

In other words, their establishment through the sympathy mechanism lends economic values the same immutability and concreteness associated with the natural world. The objectivity of the physical world has always attracted economists when searching for analogies for their own enterprise of codification. It is no coincidence that Adam Smith himself was a great admirer of Isaac Newton and the author of a *History of Astronomy*.[14] The fact that the same economic notions considered as 'evident' *ex post*, are perfectly arbitrary *ex ante,* does not affect the epistemological and methodological implications of this procedure.[15] Instead, Smith strengthens their status as proper subjects for scientific inquiry by insisting repeatedly on the fact that their establishment through social processes is driven by deep-seated unconscious motivations – such as the desire for social recognition – that are removed from the perturbing influences of an uncertain individual conscience (see also section 4.1 '"Efficient causes" and "final causes": the working of the invisible hand').

Retaining the sympathy mechanism as the only generator of value, Adam Smith also poses the basis for the distinction between positive and normative economics. When economics studies the objects whose values are evident for all economic agents, and thus exchange value, then it pursues a positive approach. When instead it studies the values and ideas resulting from constructivist rationality and outside of this inter-subjective consensus, then it pursues a normative approach.

One needs to recall the audacity of this step. The founding act accomplished by *The Wealth of Nations* does not consist of the more or less diligent elaboration of a series of pertinent practical and theoretical observations about the economic world. Such observations, many of them just as pertinent, have always been made and are contingent on their context, time and place. Certain commentators, such as Joseph Schumpeter or Murray Rothbard have even maintained that Smith's contributions to economics were inferior to those of some of his contemporaries.[16] So what? It is not that these critics, even if uncharitable, are necessarily wrong on this or that detail. Instead, they completely miss the point. The essential contribution of Adam Smith was to make the step from a descriptive to an analytical approach in economics and to provide the informational and psychological model to go with it. Of course, Adam Smith's contribution to economic theory can be criticised. However, any criticism needs to address the underlying model itself as well as its informational, social and theoretical implications rather than any fine points concerning its application to economic practice.

Smith's historical contribution is to have elaborated a world where the question of what it takes to improve one's situation is no longer relevant. Economic betterment and greater social recognition are the result of optimising the acquisition of comparable and quantifiable goods that have been fully and exhaustively codified. Where uncertainty exists, it has the informational structure of what Frank Knight in his famous dichotomy calls 'risk' (Knight 1921: 255). It can thus be quantified and internalised in simple cost-benefit calculus. Irreducible and disruptive 'uncertainty' instead is absent from *The Wealth of Nations.*

With the total codification of all economic values, Adam Smith leads his readers in fact to the doorstep of a Walrasian world. Of course, nowhere in *The Wealth of Nations* will one find a matrix of perfect markets with an identical number of columns and rows guaranteeing equilibrium and optimality. Smith always pays attention to real-life market imperfections and transaction costs even when arguing for their gradual elimination. However, his decisive contribution remains the definitive distinction between true economic values codified by the sympathy mechanism on the one hand and less evident and vaguer values introduced by government interference, economic adventurism, speculative phantasms, human ignorance, externalities, uncertainty and transaction costs on the other. Even if the term is not used by Adam Smith himself, the *ceteris paribus* clause, the distinction between economic variables and mere disturbances, finds a powerful justification in his work. This distinction justifies the beneficial results of the invisible hand as it justifies the optimality of a set of perfect markets in a Walrasian world. Jean-Pierre Dupuy remarks rightly that … the formal model of neoclassical theory (general equilibrium) is … in perfect continuity with the one developed in *TMS*' (Dupuy 1992: 105, our translation).[17]

The definitive conceptual distinction between economic and non-economic values on the basis of an elaborated communicational and psychological model is the decisive contribution of Smith's work. Acting on economic values advances the social system towards a state we would call today 'equilibrium', while acting on non-economic values retards this very progress due to its complex, open, political, and, therefore, non-codified, character. This is why the project of an economic *science* begins with *The Wealth of Nations*. One may or may not adhere to this project. One may doubt the ultimate validity of the separation of economic from non-economic values for durable human well-being as well as for an adequate representation of actual social life. However, the importance of the decisive contribution that Adam Smith's work makes to the project of an economic science should no longer be in doubt.

We shall see in Chapter 4 how the working of the invisible hand also depends crucially on the clear definition and stability of all values and behaviour. It is troubled in its task by any form of constructivist rationality attempting to transcend the social consensus formed around the values codified by the sympathy mechanism and thus hampering the socially beneficial quest for individual profit. The semantic closure inherent in the sympathy mechanism is constitutive of an economic science seeking its autonomy from neighbouring disciplines interested in the workings of society such as history, political science, sociology or ethics. This semantic closure instead lies at the heart of the intimacy of economics with jurisprudence. In indicating with the sympathy mechanism a coherent process for the formation of codified economic values and in exploring its consequences, Adam Smith has become the founding father of economic science.

3 The vertical world of the impartial spectator

3.1 The names of Adam's father: looking for the impartial spectator

In addition to the sympathy mechanism, there exists in the *Theory of Moral Sentiments* a second normative principle for organising human values and behaviour. In certain instances, it even dominates the sympathy mechanism. Given that this principle is structured around a hierarchical relationship with an authority whose precise nature remains to be determined, one may qualify it as a 'vertical' principle in opposition to the 'horizontal' sympathy mechanism. It appears only at the end of the first third of the book, following the extensive presentation of the sympathy mechanism. Then, however, it appears in a dizzying succession of different incarnations. The neutral expression of a 'vertical principle' was also chosen to highlight the dangers of a premature identification or sentimentalisation of an entity for which Adam Smith himself has great difficulty in finding a definitive name. In the secondary literature, the term 'impartial spectator' has established itself as a common reference for this vertical principle. We shall adhere to this custom in the following in order to facilitate the reader's task. However, one needs to be ever mindful that the term 'impartial spectator' is just one of a multitude of designations, and perhaps not even the most representative one, that Adam Smith employs in *The Theory of Moral Sentiments* in order to refer to this vertical principle.

Below we reproduce a selection of the expressions used by Adam Smith to designate the authority from which emanates the normative rules of the vertical dimension. The diversity of these expressions and the breadth of meaning they cover indicate, both, the difficulty to seize precisely the focal point of this vertical principle and the intensity of the effort to arrive there nevertheless:

> 'The spectator
> the impartial spectator
> the fair and impartial spectator
> the supposed impartial and well-informed spectator
> the abstract and ideal spectator of our sentiments and conduct
> the Author
> the Author of nature
> the great Director of Nature
> the great Judge of hearts
> the great judge and arbiter
> the supreme judge
> the tribunal of conscience
> this great tribunal
> the tribunal established in their breasts
> the man within the breast
> the demigod within the breast
> the man within
> the judge within
> the great inmate
> this inmate of the breast
> the inhabitant of the breast
> the great demigod within the breast
> those viceregents of God within us
> reason, principle, conscience
> this abstract man
> the Deity
> the substitute of the Deity
> the great arbiter of conduct
> this supreme arbiter of conduct
> the great arbiter and judge of conduct
> God
> the Lord our God
> that divine Being
> a divine artist
> that great, benevolent, and all-wise Being
> the great Director of the Universe
> the great Superintendent of the universe
> the all-seeing Judge of the world, whose eyes can never be deceived, and whose judgement can never be perverted.'

Despite the fact that the impartial spectator is regularly discussed in the secondary literature, his other designations are only very rarely mentioned despite their profusion throughout the text. Only Jacob Viner, here as elsewhere of irreproachable diligence, had already remarked on the multiplication of designations in his classic article 'Adam Smith and Laissez faire' (1928, 1989):

> The many titles by which this beneficent nature is designated must have taxed severely the terminological resources of the Scotch optimistic theists. Among them are "the great Director of Nature", "the final cause", "the Author of Nature", "the great judge of hearts", "an invisible hand", "Providence", "the divine Being," and, in rare instances, "God".
>
> (Viner 1928, 1989: 121)

It is quite understandable why the secondary literature historically preferred to concentrate solely on the expression 'impartial spectator'. In fact, the vast majority of commentators only read *The Theory of Moral Sentiments* after *The Wealth of Nations.* This usually implies an automatic focus on the sympathy mechanism and its reciprocity of regards with its natural proximity to the establishment of a market society. In the following, the 'impartial spectator' becomes thus just a double, a synthesis of the 'spectators', the peers with whom the Smithian individual maintains the complex relationship of imitation, jealousy and competition described above (see, for instance, Dupuy 1988, Diatkine 1991 or Dermange 2003). Other terms, such as 'the Director of nature' would have avoided such confusion but would have required the willingness to expose oneself to the tensions of the complete text rather than to find reassurance in a linear but partial interpretation.[1]

The organisation of the text of *The Theory of Moral Sentiments* can comfort such a prejudice. The impartial spectator is introduced only *after* the sympathy mechanism has been carefully introduced and exemplified in the first third of the book. In addition, it is tempting to oppose the disconcerting multiplication of the designations of the impartial spectator with the elegant clarity of the exposition of the sympathy mechanism. Any reader in search of a single, easily communicable meaning of the text would thus be inclined to consider the impartial spectator just an annex of the first principle. In its vast majority – notable exceptions are Raphael 1975 and Brown 1994 – the secondary literature on Adam Smith, which is however of a stupefying variety, thus does not accord to the impartial spectator the status of an independent organising principle. This approach regrettably deprives Smith's work of an essential dimension. It is also the sign of a selective reading since Adam Smith repeatedly and explicitly asserts the existence of the impartial spectator as the source of an autonomous normative framework.[2]

The proliferation of expressions employed by Adam Smith to target the source of the vertical principle sketches in a preliminary and uncertain manner, an all-knowing and all-powerful authority with divine attributes that unconditionally imposes its laws. Protean and elusive, this entity is everywhere and nowhere. The impossibility to fix a definitive name for this authority endowed with divine attributes, whose presence is nevertheless manifest at all times, recalls an earlier, similar account. It recalls God's refusal to communicate to Moses a name pronounceable by humans in the book *Exodus*:

> And Moses said unto God, Behold, when I come unto the children of Israel, and shall say unto them, The God of your fathers hath sent me unto you; and they shall say to me, what is his name? What shall I say unto them? And God said unto Moses, I AM THAT I AM: and he said, thus shall thou say unto the children of Israel, I AM hath sent me unto you.
>
> (*The Bible*, "Exodus", Chapter 3, 13–14)

One has to consider the impossibility to name 'the one that is' in parallel with the interdiction to represent God's image. Fixing God's image or name in a form that is pronounceable by humans would imply a limitation to his almightiness and ubiquity. In a similar way, the fact that the impartial spectator cannot be pinpointed in any definite manner is also proof of the immediacy and all-pervasiveness of his presence in Adam Smith. And yet, the impartial spectator under all his different designations in *The Theory of Moral Sentiments* is not simply the Christian God. Adam Smith's relationship with religion is more ambivalent than that and the impartial spectator is at the same time more abstract *and* more present in everyday decisions than in traditional Christian religion. On the other hand, there is no doubt that the figure impartial spectator carries a good deal of religious heritage with it (see below).

Power and limits of the vertical principle: the two tribunals

Already in 1975, one of the best-known experts on Adam Smith, David D. Raphael, co-editor of the definitive 'Glasgow edition' of *The Theory of Moral Sentiments* (1976), underlined that the values identified with the impartial spectator are different from those arising from the sympathy mechanism:

'The "impartial spectator", "the man within", may judge differently from the actual spectator, "the man without" … It is easy to miss this distinction and to suppose that conscience for Smith is purely a reflection of actual social attitudes'(Raphael 1975: 90).

In order to substantiate this distinction, Raphael cites the letter of 10th October 1759 (the year of the publication of *The Theory of Moral Sentiments*) that Adam Smith wrote to his friend George Elliott. In this letter, Smith spells out his intention to maintain two independent normative principles in *The Theory of Moral Sentiments*:

> … [this] is intended both to confirm my Doctrine that our judgements concerning our own conduct have always a reference to the sentiments of some other being, and to shew [sic] that, notwithstanding this, real magnanimity and conscious virtue can support itselfe [sic] under the disapprobation of all mankind.
>
> (Raphael 1975: 91)

Raphael's demonstration of the existence of two independent normative principles, however, remained largely confidential. The silence of the majority of commentators on this point is difficult to explain given the obviousness and clarity of the text on this point. It is as if the sympathy mechanism took its revenge by having commentators and critics shape their perceptions by regarding each other rather than by concentrating on their individual readings of the text. As elsewhere, also in the history of ideas the currency of a socially codified exchange value circulates more easily than new and unproven work requiring additional investment from the reader. Facts, however, can be pernickety and Adam Smith clearly does postulate the existence of an autonomous normative entity and writes in the chapter programmatically called 'Of the Influences and Authority of Conscience':

> It is a stronger power, a more forcible motive, which exerts itself upon such occasions. It is reason, principle, conscience, the inhabitant of the breast, the man within, the great judge and arbiter of our conduct. It is he who, whenever we are about to act so as to affect the happiness of others, calls to us, with a voice capable of astonishing the most presumptuous of our passions, that we are but one of the multitude … It is from him only that we learn the real littleness of ourselves, and of whatever relates to ourselves,

> and the natural misrepresentations of self-love can be corrected only by the eye of this impartial spectator. It is he who shows us the propriety of generosity and the deformity of injustice; the propriety of resigning the greatest interests of our own, for the yet greater interest of others … .
>
> (Smith 1759 (III.3.4): 158)

First, the passage just quoted presents the impartial spectator as a norm-setting force independent of the sympathy mechanism, whose very *raison d'être* is to generate 'self-love' through mutual recognition. Second, the passage also introduces the two cardinal virtues associated with this force: generosity (in other passages frequently referred to as 'benevolence') and justice. Generosity and benevolence need to be clearly distinguished from sympathy. We have already seen that the key virtues associated with the sympathy mechanism are prudence and propriety. Prudence and propriety imply actions coherent with public opinion and social norms established by the sympathy mechanism. Directly or indirectly, by way of a detour through personal wealth acquisition, they will lead to public acceptance and approbation. Benevolence instead will lead to acts of disinterested kindness and altruism demanding nothing better than the approbation of the impartial spectator. It is related to the notion of 'charity'. At no point will it seek satisfying a social morality and it can even constitute a perturbing element for the conventional social bond.

The Smithian system of values is further characterised by the fact that the two distinct normative principles respectively emanating from the impartial spectator and the sympathy mechanism apply to two different spheres, or rather levels, of human life. There exist, in fact, two courts or tribunals, which assess human actions:

> But though man has … been rendered the immediate judge of mankind, he has been rendered so only in the first instance; and an appeal lies from his sentence to a much higher tribunal, to the tribunal of their own consciences, to that of the supposed impartial and well-informed spectator, to that of the man within the breast, the great arbiter and judge of their conduct. The jurisdictions of those two tribunals are founded upon principles which though in some respects resembling and akin, are, however, in reality different and distinct. The jurisdiction of the man without, is founded altogether in the desire of actual praise, and in the aversion to actual blame. The jurisdiction of the man within, is founded

> altogether in the desire of praise-worthiness, and in the aversion to blame-worthiness … .
>
> (Smith 1759 (III.2.32): 150)

Thus there exist two tribunals, two distinct normative instances to assess human behaviour. The first is of human nature, the second belongs to the impartial spectator. The separating line between them is defined by the distinction between 'praise' (for what *is* appreciated by humans) and 'praise-worthiness' (for what *should* be appreciated by humans). The economist may want to seek here the roots of the distinction between subjective exchange value and objective use value but this is not necessary to appreciate the argument. Adam Smith, for instance, applies this distinction in his critique of Epicure, of whom he disapproves for putting too much emphasis on superficial flattery and not enough on true merit (Smith 1759 (VII.II.2.13): 352). And while Smith concedes that the distinction between these two spheres is not always easy to make, he never doubts its existence as such:

> The respect which we feel for wisdom and virtue is, no doubt, different from that which we conceive for wealth and greatness; and it requires no very nice discernment to distinguish the difference … In some particular features they are, no doubt, different, but, in the general air of the countenance, they seem to be so very nearly the same, that inattentive observers are very apt to mistake them the one for the other.
>
> (Smith 1759 (I.III.3.3): 73)

The paradoxical nature of the Smithian synthesis (see Chapter 4) is foreshadowed in the complex relationship that the two courts of opinion maintain with each other. Even if the judgement of the impartial spectator is considered as 'much higher', its influence is in fact radically limited. In case of conflict between the two judgements, the tribunal of the impartial spectator possesses a purely abstract superiority, which does not limit the autonomy of the tribunal of men in practice. Following the injunctions emanating from the impartial spectator does not provide licence for avoiding the constraints of the norms formatted by the sympathy mechanism.

Another crucial distinction between the two tribunals is that the tribunal of the impartial spectator judges intentions, while the tribunal of men judges actions. In a first approach, Smith argues engagingly that only the quality of the intentions determines the true merit or blameworthiness of an action. Subsequently, however, he underlines the fragility of such a normative criterion in daily life. This leads him ultimately to conclude that intentions should have no influence at all on human judgements, which should remain restricted to verifiable facts:

> Actions, therefore which either produce actual evil, or attempt to produce it, and thereby put us in the immediate fear of it, are by the Author of nature rendered the only proper and approved objects of human punishment and resentment. Sentiments, designs, affections, though it is from these that according to cool reason human actions derive their whole merit or demerit, are placed by the great Judge of hearts beyond the limits of every human jurisdiction, and are reserved for the cognizance of his own unerring tribunal.
>
> (Smith 1759 (II.3.2): 124)

The fact that the 'Author of nature' himself operates this distinction highlights the whole complexity of Smith's construction. The Author of nature in fact intervenes on two levels. On the first level, the 'great Judge of hearts', one of his many aliases, is indeed the immediate reference for judging human intentions directly. On the second level, the Author of nature *himself* decides that humans should limit themselves to judging facts or actions. Two forms of justice thus emanate from the impartial spectator, the first directly, the second indirectly. We shall see below that a simplified, codified and operationalised version of the second form of justice also structures market society and polices inter-human relations where necessary. This indirect form of justice will indeed accompany the pursuit of a prudent and socially formatted self-interest. The Author of nature thus always has two routes at his disposal to achieve his objectives which remain general welfare and the propagation of the species. The defining characteristic of the Smithian œuvre, which has contributed to numerous misunderstandings, is that the second, indirect route is considered safer and that the direct route is thus explicitly forsaken.

Adam Smith loves nothing better than to perambulate in the many twists and turns of this double argumentation. Having firmly argued that only actions can constitute the objects of human justice, he returns to his first observation that only intentions – which are outside the province of mere human judges – determine an action's true merit. Smith is particularly interested in cases where crimes have been committed unintentionally or even unconsciously. Culpability or guilt become very ambivalent notions in this process. 'Evil which is done without design should be regarded as a misfortune to the doer as well as to the sufferer' (Smith 1759 (II.III.3.4): 125) he thus asserts. This ambivalence attains its climax in the passage where Smith comments on the tragedy of King Oedipus and qualifies the sense of guilt of Oedipus and his mother Jocasta as 'fallacious', since they committed their incestuous crime unconscious of their biological relationship:

> The distress which an innocent person feels, who, by some accident, has been led to do something which, if it had been done with knowledge and design would have justly exposed him to the deepest reproach, has given occasion to some of the finest and most interesting scenes both of the ancient and of the modern drama. It is this fallacious sense of guilt, if I may call it so, which constitutes the whole distress of Oedipus and Jocasta … They are all of them in the highest sense piacular, though not one of them is in the smallest degree guilty.
>
> (Smith 1759 (II.III.3.5): 126)

The divergence between the two levels of justice is here expressed in the opposition of the two qualifying adjectives 'piacular' and 'guilty', the first belonging to the sphere of the divine and the second belonging to the sphere of humans.

The possibility of behaviour that is 'highly piacular', but innocent as far as any real-world consequences are concerned, reinforces the incompatibility of the sphere of the impartial spectator and the human sphere structured by the sympathy mechanism. The conundrum is double. First, in the concrete world of human existence there exists no possibility to atone for such piacular behaviour. Second, why bring sacrifices for expiation, if there are no consequences other then the disapproval of the impartial spectator? Only in a paragraph added in the sixth and last edition of *The Theory of Moral Sentiments* that appeared in 1796, does Adam Smith explain that a man who has become piacular – for example, by violating a religious sanctuary – also owes expiation and reparation in proportion of the severity of the crime in this world, even when it has been committed without intent or due to ignorance (Smith 1759 (II.3.4): 167).

Such commensurability would, in principle, allow for a direct transition between the sphere of human actions and the sphere of divine approval and forgiveness. However, this is not the principal route chosen by Adam Smith. Throughout *The Theory of Moral Sentiments* and *The Wealth of Nations*, he employs the more elaborate argument that the pursuit of wealth, characterised by the acceptance of interpersonal values and the submission under human laws is a safer, even if roundabout, way towards happiness. The link between the world of the impartial spectator and the world of the sympathy mechanism is thus constructed in the form of an indirect synthesis (see Chapter 4).

As far as the myth of King Oedipus is concerned, conformity with society's penal and moral laws saves the individual from any overt sanctions for 'unconscious' crimes or crimes of intention. The inevitable separation from the sphere of the impartial spectator this implies, however, accounts for the air of melancholy that, from then on, hovers over the life of the Smithian individual for whom 'the very suspicion of a fatherless world, must be the most melancholy of all reflections' (Smith 1759 (VI.II.3.2): 277). At a general level, the invisible hand will, of course, continue to ensure that individual wealth maximisation, as the purest form of social conformity, realises His objectives. Only at the most abstract level, can the Smithian individual consider himself still in concord with the Director of nature, once the strict separation between the two tribunals has been enacted.

On the difference in status of 'Generosity' and 'Justice'

It would, however, be premature to write off any direct consideration of the vertical dimension structured around the impartial spectator as a purely optional embellishment for an elite in search of particular sensations. Throughout *The Theory of Moral Sentiments* and in several passages of *The Wealth of Nations*, Adam Smith insists on the human costs of abandoning an active ethical search. Coming back to the distinction between actions and intentions, he depicts the characters of a friend who remains inwardly cold towards a benefactor and of a wife who has lost the love for her husband. Their inner 'intentions' – the sphere of the impartial spectator – are characterised as imperfect and are pointed out as being at the root of a number of omissions in daily intercourse. However, their behaviour is considered as perfectly acceptable as long as each of them comports him- or herself correctly, that is in accordance with existing social norms, towards their respective partners. Such conformity with social expectations is, according to Smith, the only applicable standard, even if the shortcomings of their behaviour are blatantly evident:

> Such a friend and such a wife are, neither of them, undoubtedly, the very best of their kinds … they will fail in many nice and delicate regards, they will miss many opportunities in obliging,

> which they could never have overlooked if they had possessed the sentiment that is proper to their situation. Though not the very first of their kinds, however, they are perhaps the second ... None but those of the happiest mould are capable ... of acting upon all occasions with the most delicate and accurate propriety. The coarse clay of which the bulk of mankind are formed, cannot be wrought up to such perfection. There is scarce any man, however, who by discipline, education, and example, may not be so impressed with a regard to general rules, as to act upon almost every occasion with tolerable decency, and through the whole of his life to avoid any considerable degree of blame.
>
> (Smith 1759 (III.5.1): 188–89)

The phrase 'the coarse clay of which the bulk of mankind are formed' has become the emblem for Adam Smith's pragmatic empiricism. It highlights his fondness for establishing the 'middling', everyday conduct of real people as the appropriate standard for judging human behaviour as opposed to the world of ideals and intentions associated with the impartial spectator. Friend and wife behave without enthusiasm but correctly and thus escape censure. Their lack of generosity and love may be deplored but they will not be held to account for their omissions. The passage prefigures the distinction between a positive and a normative approach in the study of human behaviour. The expectations of the impartial spectator of behaviour coherent with true feelings and intentions are normative. Behaviour in accordance with social norms codified by the sympathy mechanism is a positive fact. And if in doubt, when direct opposition between the two reference frameworks becomes inevitable, Adam Smith will come down on the side of a positive study of actual behaviour. Already earlier he had remarked 'that the present inquiry is not concerning a matter of right, if I may say so, but concerning a matter of fact' (Smith 1759 (II.I.5.10): 90).

However, limiting oneself only to this account would mean underestimating the sophistication of the interaction between positive and normative elements in Adam Smith's work. First, the 'positive' behaviour based on existing social conventions acquires, even if imperfect, its own legitimacy. In its turn, this legitimacy evolves into a new set of norms in Adam Smith's work, stricter and more absolute than any other. This new and *immanent* normativity is the result of auto-organisation on the basis of the sympathy mechanism. The point is thus not simply substituting one set of exogenous norms for another set of norms, but more importantly substituting one process for the generation of norms, the dialogue with the impartial spectator, for another process, the sympathy mechanism.

Second and even more importantly, the real and imperfect world of sympathising traders and craftsmen continues to maintain crucial links to the ideal world of the impartial spectator. This double nature of the relationship between the two spheres – which nevertheless remains clearly distinguishable at all times – has been a major obstacle to fully appreciating Smith's work. The key link is constituted by the notion of *justice*, an absolute norm that is largely exogenous to the processes of auto-organisation, and yet interferes in a very concrete manner with the daily life of the participants in these processes. One could argue that the laws a society chooses to give itself result from self-referential processes of auto-organisation, even if these specific processes might operate on longer timeframes. However, Adam Smith does not present matters in this way. We may recall that justice and beneficence were the two virtues associated with the impartial spectator. Among the two, Smith operates a clear distinction with respect to their relative importance. Beneficence or generosity becomes, in a 'normal' society, that is a society that is the object of positive study, simply a personal option. Justice instead is indispensable in absolutely every circumstance for maintaining a given social order and even social life in general. 'Society may subsist, though not in the most comfortable state, without beneficence; but the prevalence of injustice must utterly destroy it'(Smith 1759 (II.II.3.3): 101).

The two virtues associated with the impartial spectator do not carry the same weight. And having compared beneficence with a beautiful architectural ornament, Adam Smith concludes that 'Justice, on the contrary, is the main pillar that upholds the whole edifice' (Smith 1759 (II.II.3.4): 101).

We know that Adam Smith, the man, did not deprive himself of engaging in the aristocratic virtue of beneficence, giving large sums to institutions of public welfare (Rae 1895: 10). Nevertheless, it is evident that the economist considered exercising this virtue a personal option and not an obligation necessary for maintaining the social fabric. On the other hand, Adam Smith repeatedly states that upholding justice is an indispensable condition for enabling any form of social life and never ever questions this conclusion. This clarity of position is all the more remarkable in a text characterised by a surfeit of exemptions, qualifications and careful trade-offs. The importance of justice results from the fact that it is, together with the sympathy mechanism, a vital rampart against the destructive force of the passions. And if the sympathy mechanism remains 'contaminated' by the passions in the expression of Jean-Pierre Dupuy, justice is the ultimate, non-negotiable barrier against the violent egotism of the passions.

And yet, the concept of justice remains difficult to grasp. In *The Theory of Moral Sentiments*, Smith never specifies a concrete legal provision, even if one can indirectly infer certain elements (see below). Most of the time, justice remains 'flat' and pure form. We have already seen that Adam Smith likens justice to a *grammar* of human behaviour and other virtues to the art of rhetoric (Smith 1759 (III.6.11): 205).

Justice for Smith has no other function than rendering the organisation or auto-organisation of social life *possible*. In no case does he want 'justice' to substitute itself for this organisation. His objective is to establish a minimal set of norms that guarantee the sustainability of society. The final form of society is not the object of justice, which should not pursue any precise ethical or moral intentions. Once social life has been rendered possible through the observation of justice, the community of men will establish its own structure on the basis of alternative processes such as the sympathy mechanism. Justice is thus supposed to consist of rules that are perfectly clear, general and independent of any specific social context or interpretation. This distinguishes justice from other obligations, such as the duty to show gratitude, which depends on particular circumstances and the personal appreciation of the actors involved:

> There is, however one virtue of which the general rules determine with the greatest exactness every external action which it requires. This virtue is justice. The rules of justice are accurate in the highest degree, and admit of no exceptions or modifications …
>
> (Smith 1759 (III.6.10): 203–4)

For Adam Smith, the rules of justice are characterised by an absence of any positive content. Their principal function is to channel the destructive force of the passions at a very basic level. Consequently, the notion of justice is often easier to grasp when considering its absence, as is the case at the very end of *The Theory of Moral Sentiments*

> As the violation of justice is what men will never submit to from one another, the public magistrate is under necessity of employing the power of the commonwealth to enforce the practice of this virtue.
>
> (Smith 1759 (VII.IV.36): 402–3)

The violation of justice or its contempt is perceived almost instinctively as an aggression, even when it is quite impossible to indicate which precise legal provision was not respected. The revolt against any form of real or perceived injustice must, however, not transform itself into violent chaos, where each man takes justice into his own hands. The state must therefore take responsibility for maintaining justice by reserving the monopoly of physical violence for itself. This is even its main function. In final consequence, in the set-up devised by Adam Smith, specific legal provisions have no other function than to ensure their respect. The absolute and indiscriminate respect that justice commands is indeed close to the Hobbesian relativism expressed in the formula that 'there are no unjust laws'. For Adam Smith, as far as justice is concerned, the spirit of the Law of the impartial spectator is to follow human laws to the letter, independently of their content.

Knud Haakonssen thus qualifies justice in the Smithian world quite rightly as a 'negative virtue' that does not aim at substituting itself for other virtues (Haakonssen 1998: 169). He cites, on this occasion, Smith himself:

> Mere justice is, upon most occasions, but a negative virtue, and only hinders us from hurting our neighbour … We may often fulfil all the rules of justice by sitting still and doing nothing.
>
> (Smith 1759 (II.II.1.9): 95–96)

Haakonssen also draws attention to the distinction that Smith makes between *laws of justice* and *laws of police*, two concepts that are roughly compatible with the modern concepts of penal law and civil law (Smith 1759 (VII.IV.37): 404). Obviously, only the laws of justice correspond to justice proper; that is the form of non-negotiable 'natural justice', which is closely associated with the impartial spectator.

The laws of the second category, the 'laws of police', or more comprehensively, the 'laws of police, revenue and arms', are concerned with the actual organisation of society and might very well be shaped through the sympathy mechanism. They depend on time, place and public opinion even if the rhythm of arriving at converging conceptions might be somewhat slower than the rhythms of the sympathy processes that define the passing fads of fashion. Smith clearly links the laws of police to the organisation of market society as presented in the *Wealth of Nations* when he writes in the preface of the 6th edition of *The Theory of Moral Sentiments*:

> In the last paragraph of the first Edition of the present work, I said, that I should in another discourse endeavour to give an account of the general principles of law and government, and of

> the different revolutions which they had undergone in the different ages and periods of society; not only in what concerns justice, but in what concerns police, revenue and arms, and whatever else is the object of law. In the Enquiry concerning the Nature and Causes of the Wealth Nations, I have partly executed this promise; at least so far as concerns police, revenue, and arms.
>
> (Smith 1759 (Advertisement): 3–4)[3]

The 'laws of justice' instead are concerned exclusively with torts in a perfectly general fashion, without any consideration of context. Their actual content is difficult to fathom, but the synthesis provided by François Dermange on the basis of scattered remarks and allusions is quite convincing. Justice would thus concern ' … the defence of life and of physical and moral integrity, the defence of property and finally the enforcement of promises (Dermange 2003: 119, our translation). While the concept of 'moral integrity' is somewhat complex – we will come back to it in the discussion of the government's role in providing primary education – Dermange's brief synthesis renders well the minimal but indispensable programme behind the notion of justice in Adam Smith's work.

Dermange is also correct in introducing the Aristotelian distinction between commutative and distributive justice, the first referring to the rules of exchange and the second to distribution proper. In effect, for Smith, 'justice' is essentially commutative justice. Pursuing a notion of distributive justice instead would fall into the domain of beneficence or generosity. Doing so might be desirable from an ethical point of view or a sign of personal distinction, but it can never be the subject of a legal obligation: 'Even the most ordinary degree of kindness or beneficence … cannot, among equals, be extorted by force' (Smith 1759 (II.II.1.7): 94). Finally, justice for Adam Smith also defines the separation between the public sphere, where it operates, and the private sphere. It is in public and during social interaction that justice needs to bind any overbearing passions that have escaped the normalising force of the sympathy mechanism. Structuring the passions in private cannot be the subject of any man-made laws.

Justice in *The Theory of Moral Sentiments* and *The Wealth of Nations* is thus a set of non-negotiable rules that guarantees the essential ability of society to function. They are non-negotiable but remain 'open' in the sense that they escape easy codification. The preservation of physical integrity, the protection of the individual as an essential building block of society is, however, always an indispensable element. Justice, as the principal heritage of the impartial spectator in a world dominated by economic exchange, is characterised by the protection it provides to the most essential elements of human existence rather than by its ambition to shape social life itself.

This 'lean' character of justice goes hand in hand with the diffidence that Adam Smith harbours against all concentrations of power. His intent to limit economic power in the case of state monopolies has already been mentioned. And although government is charged with enforcing justice, Smith is averse to making it a new centre of excessive power. The more government prerogatives are limited, the better it is, given that government is always in danger of being taken over by special interests. More often than not, they are in search of economic monopoly. Smith thus distrusts any 'positive' legislation that would stipulate and enforce certain conducts or outcomes. Any such legislation would, in fact, be contingent on time and place and would only substitute itself for the results of the process of auto-organisation that is the sympathy mechanism. While it would deserve the respect that any law, or any social convention for that matter, deserves, it would not be part of justice proper:

> Systems of positive law, therefore, though they deserve the greatest authority, as the records of the sentiments of mankind in different ages and nations, yet can never be regarded as accurate systems of the rules of natural justice.
>
> (Smith 1759 (VII.IV.36)

Despite this principal reservation regarding positive laws, there can be no doubt that unflinching observation of *any* legal provision in practice is a hallmark of Smith's vision of society. This holds for both *The Theory of Moral Sentiments* and *The Wealth of Nations*. Nevertheless, in the transition between the two books, several changes in nuance can be observed. First, we observe the evolution from a contemplation of abstract principles to a discussion of concrete legal provisions. Second, the reference point for justice is no longer the elusive impartial spectator but actual government, except in a number of important but isolated exceptions (see also Chapter 5 'The ethics of morality'). The abstract authority demanding the unconditional observance of the Law has been replaced by a concrete social imperative demanding the diligent observation of human laws in order to allow society to function. Justice thus allows the transcendental and vertical instance of the impartial spectator to become immanent to the horizontal world of humans. The notion of justice thus plays a crucial role in the Smithian setup. It constitutes, in fact, the principal transition between the two spheres and thus the most important legacy of the impartial spectator in the secularised world of *The Wealth of Nations*.

The attentive reader of *The Wealth of Nations* will also make the distinction between the point of view of the author himself and the point of view he requires from the individual economic agent. The author, very explicitly, reserves for himself the right to criticise, quite severely where he deems necessary, specific administrative or legal provisions formulated by government. However, these same provisions are considered to be an invariable reality for each economic actor. A law can be critically judged from the point of view of the economist, but it is not individually negotiable. Only in one single instance and in very qualified terms does Adam Smith permit himself to defend the delinquent against the law he has violated. When presenting the case of smugglers trying to circumvent high import taxes on luxury goods, Smith writes:

> ... the hope of evading such taxes by smuggling gives frequent occasion to forfeitures and other penalties, which entirely ruin the smuggler; a person, who, though no doubt highly blameable for violating the laws of his country, is frequently incapable of violating those of natural justice, and would have been, in every respect, an excellent citizen, had not the laws of his country made that a crime which nature never meant to be so.
>
> (Smith 1776 (II.V.2.2.4): 429)

The passage, by the way, also revives the distinction between 'natural justice' and 'laws of police, revenue and arms', where the smuggler has only violated the latter. Generally, however, this conflict is no longer discussed in *The Wealth of Nations*, where the latter usually count as imperfect, but indispensable expressions of the former.

Only in three further passages, which all concern restrictions on the free choice of profession (Smith 1776 (I.10.2): 133; (IV.5): 548 and (IV.9): 712–13) does Smith underline the conflict between concrete legal provisions and natural liberty. In these cases, laws restricting the pursuit of self-interest in conformity with natural liberty are clearly identified as economically harmful and presented as such by the economist-author. Never, however, does he suggest breaking the laws in order to further the economic objectives harmonising with natural liberty; not in the cited passages and even less so in the rest of the book.

However, the economist does not address the individual economic agent – who remains obliged to follow even economically senseless laws to the letter – but the sovereign decision-maker, that is government. In this perspective, Smith has no reservations about expressing himself clearly. The great theme of *The Wealth of Nations* is that unrestricted auto-organisation on the basis of the pursuit of individual self-interest yields superior outcomes to governmental attempts to enforce particular forms of organisation. Government thus needs to restrict itself to the very minimalist programme of justice consisting of (1) the protection against internal and external aggression, (2) the enforcement of contracts and (3) the limited provision of certain public goods such as primary education. And yet, one of the two central requests of the impartial spectator survives intact. This distinguishes the observation of justice from the practice of generosity. Even if *The Wealth of Nations* stays generally far away from any direct invocation of the unnameable Director of nature, with the notion of justice, a central part of his heritage survives: economic liberalism requires the diligent observation of all laws, any law, whatever it may say. Highlighting the imperfections, restrictions and perverse effects of these laws is the privilege of the economist but is not part of the prerogatives of the individual economic actor.

Justice thus constitutes the lasting heritage of the impartial spectator even at a moment when Adam Smith no longer considers his direct influence on daily human behaviour as decisive. And while the pursuit of justice is clearly a central demand of the impartial spectator, it is but a part of his complete function. On the basis of this insight we can now attempt to draw a fuller picture of this elusive normative instance with its multiple invocations.

The nature of the impartial spectator

The impartial spectator exists. He exists in *The Theory of Moral Sentiments* as a clearly identified autonomous normative instance. He survives in *The Wealth of Nations* in the 'orthogonalised' form of human laws and as the force that may, on rare occasions, override the imperative of the individual pursuit of maximum wealth. Who is he then? Is he a God, the Christian God perhaps, a benevolent, universal force, conscience, the idea of a father whom Adam Smith has never known?

Religion seems a promising route, given that Smith several times refers to the instance we have chosen for convenience to call the impartial spectator as 'God'. Adam Smith's religiosity is indeed a topic that is regularly addressed in the secondary literature (see, for instance, Raphael 1975, Pack 1991, Evensky 2005 or Dermange (2003)). In this literature a certain consensus has established itself to consider Adam Smith as a theist, that is as someone who believes in a conscious and benevolent force at the origin of the world without necessarily believing that this force intervenes in a personalised and explicit form in everyday life.[4] An important aspect of theism – and one that makes associating Adam Smith with it attractive – is the intrinsic modesty of the ethical project for which the individual is held accountable. Men should not try to transform nature but should go on diligently about their everyday tasks without trying to understand the greater scheme of things. It is the work of God, not of men, to inscribe their activities into a larger providential plan (see, for instance, Taylor 1989).

A theist approach has two central notions. First, the final design of creation transcends human comprehension. Second, God is not present as an identifiable entity and even less so as a 'person' with human traits. This God of the theists cannot be separated from his creation and is present in all its details as a benevolent force. The first characteristic harmonises well with the function of the impartial spectator as 'final cause', unbeknownst to humans who can only perceive the 'efficient cause', which is why his hand must remain invisible (see Chapter 4 'The paradoxical synthesis'). The second characteristic, the presence of an omnipresent well-meaning force, chimes less well with an impartial spectator who poses himself in explicit contradiction with the results arising from the inter-subjective game of sympathy.

In the text of *The Theory of Moral Sentiments*, the impartial spectator also has precise traits that are far more explicit than those of the implicit God of the theists. First, he is the one who sees and knows everything, from whom there is no secret. He is also a judge, an arbiter, somebody who sets forth and enforces the law. Finally, he is the 'the demigod inside the breast', the 'great inmate'. The impartial spectator exists primarily in an interiorised form in the mind of every individual. In particular, he sees what the others, the neighbours, the peers cannot see. The impartial spectator is interested in true virtue, rather than the appearance of virtue. As we have seen above in the discussion of the two tribunals and the distinction between 'praise-worthiness' and 'praise', this is what distinguishes the judgement of the impartial spectator from the social judgements developed on the basis of the sympathy mechanism.

In fact, an individual engaged in the process of the sympathy mechanism has no means to distinguish between appearance and truth. This is the hallmark of an iconic signification, whose tenet is, as we saw, 'what you see is what you get'. In more technical terms, there is no distinction between semantic content and its representation, or between what is signified (*signifié*) and the signifier (*signifiant*). While this distinction may be of limited importance when considering objects of everyday life, it is vital when discussing fundamental questions of morality and ethics. And it is only the impartial spectator who will introduce the difference between the shell of a commonly accepted idea of propriety and the kernel of what is truly the right thing to do. He does so in an interior dialogue with each individual that is independent of social conventions or 'casuistic rules' as Smith refers to them:

> In what cases friendship ought to yield to gratitude, or gratitude to friendship; in what cases the strongest of all natural affection ought to yield to a regard for the safety of those superiors upon whose safety often depends that of the whole society; and in what cases natural affection may, without impropriety, prevail over that regard; must be left altogether to the decision of the man within the breast, the supposed impartial spectator, the great judge and arbiter of our conduct. If we place ourselves completely in his situation, if we really view ourselves with his eyes, and as he views us, and listen with diligent and reverential attention to what he suggests to us, his voice will never deceive us. We shall stand in need of no casuistic rules to direct our conduct.
>
> (Smith 1759 (VI.II.1.22): 267)

Adam Smith's position in this respect is not unalterable and evolves during the course of *The Theory of Moral Sentiments*. As we shall see in the next section, he will take position *against* the possibility of such direct communication with the impartial spectator independent of social convention in his refutation towards the end of the book of the notion of 'moral sense' propagated by his mentor and predecessor Francis Hutcheson. This refutation of direct contact with the impartial spectator will open the way for the outline of a horizontal world built exclusively on the sympathy mechanism and its logical extension, market exchange.

However, we are not there yet. While the theist hypothesis, i.e. that Smith advocated individual liberty free from ethical constraints to further the design of a distant, benevolent force, harmonises well with the ultimate strategic slant of his work, it is also incomplete. Except for the passage concerning the discussion with Hutcheson, the idea of a more demanding notion of virtue is present throughout *The Theory of Moral Sentiments* (see, in particular, chapter VI 'On the Character of Virtue'). This notion of virtue is inevitably structured around the impartial spectator who has a far too active presence at the level of individual decision-making to be subsumed into a theist approach, in which man abandons himself to his consubstantiality with a sensible universe.

Finally, we have underlined, in the introduction to Chapter 3, the analogy between the avalanche of names, all provisional, proposed by Adam Smith for the impartial spectator and God's refusal to answer Moses' question otherwise than with an imperious 'I am that I am'. There exists thus an essential attribute of the impartial spectator that approaches him to the personal God of the Judeo-Christian tradition. Nevertheless, finding a definitive answer to the question 'Who is the impartial spectator?' is undoubtedly impossible. The cause is that Adam Smith himself, for reasons that will be discussed below, would most likely have been unable to answer the question.

In addition, the religious facets of the impartial spectator mix and interweave with other facets that belong to another domain, which is traditionally considered distinct from that of religion, the domain of psychoanalysis. In the Freudian-Lacanian tradition, notions such as the 'super-ego', the 'ego-ideal' or the 'father-ideal' largely cover the same semantic field as the impartial spectator: great force, omniscience, interiorisation (and thus omnipresence) and association with the Law. The notion of an almighty but elusive father figure and, in particular, his name, 'the name of the father', can help to highlight an additional facet of the impartial spectator, namely his authority. The link between authority and the notion of 'father' is established by Adam Smith himself who notes in *The Wealth of Nations* that ' … father is the appellation of a superior; brother of an equal; and son, of an inferior' (II.V.I.2): 233).[5] Pursuing this line of thought, David D. Raphael, for example, sees the impartial spectator as an instance of the super-ego:

> Adam Smith's theory can certainly stand comparison with the best known of modern psychological explanations of conscience, Freud's account of the super-ego. This is similar to Smith's view in taking conscience to be a second self built up in the mind as a reflection of the attitudes of outside persons.
>
> (Raphael 1975: 97)

With his remarks on the impartial spectator as super-ego, Raphael offers a promising lead. This lead, however, needs to be followed up with caution, in particular with respect to the idea that the super-ego would be similar to a conscience 'built up in the mind as a reflection of the attitudes of outside persons'. Smith insists regularly on the opposing judgements of the impartial spectator and social expectations.

As we have shown above, the two also have very different informational structures that can be characterised respectively by a symbolic and an iconic form of signification. Another point is worth highlighting. According to Freud, the super-ego is an unconscious emanation of the 'id' that inhibits the individual from satisfying his desires. The impartial spectator, however, leads largely a conscious existence in the mind of the Smithian individual, even though he will ultimately disappear as the 'final cause' and guarantor of the general welfare behind the 'effective causes' of individual wealth maximisation and social approbation. Smith clearly does have a notion of unconscious motives for human behaviour. Nevertheless, the term 'super-ego' needlessly implies a closer structural relationship between the psychological systems created by Smith and Freud than is warranted. Both develop systems, in which actual human behaviour is the outcome of the conflict between individual, largely unconscious, passions or impulses, the normalising force of social life and, with varying insistence, a distinct ethical aspiration. The ultimate focus of Smith's work, however, is social life, while the ultimate focus of Freud's work is the individual. Nevertheless, a more complete study of their similarities and differences than can be developed in this essay seems a profoundly worthwhile undertaking. There are also a number of textual traces that argue in favour of a historic strand extending from Smith through Hegel and Schopenhauer to Freud. The present essay, however, restricts itself to the identification of the structural analogies between Smith and Freud on this issue.

Faithful to our initial intent to *read* Adam Smith without prejudice and to abandon any ambition to resolve all the tension his work contains, we will not offer one single interpretation of the impartial spectator. God, father-ideal, super-ego, conscience, the possible metaphorical interpretations all belong to semantic fields that maintain close relations and are less incompatible with each other than their habitual use in casual discourse implies.

The real problem lies elsewhere. Showing that Adam Smith makes repeated references to an ideal father or a God who guarantees justice does not answer the key question we presented at the beginning of this section: why does Smith not succeed in clearly naming and thus identifying the 'great Superintendent of the universe'? Let us recall that the term 'impartial spectator' was only retained for reasons of convenience and that it has no particular standing in the text. It is as if Adam Smith, in the endless series of ever-changing variations, cannot or does not want to settle on any definite 'name of the father'. Nor does he want to install him in the nameless universality of the God of Moses.

Adam Smith thus assumes a strange intermediate position, in which he turns permanently around the issue of identifying the impartial spectator but without ever providing him with the definite status of being unidentifiable.

This double inability to settle the issue of the final designation of the impartial spectator, the 'name-of-the-father', is directly related to another determining feature of Adam Smith's world – the absence of all symbolic or metaphoric signification. We have highlighted above the extent to which this absence of symbolic signification and the resulting prevalence of iconic signification reduces communicational transaction costs and thus enables the construction of a market society. There exists, in fact, a strong link between the absence of a symbolic function and the problem to find the name of the 'impartial spectator'. The French psychoanalyst and theorist Jacques Lacan has perhaps most clearly expressed this link by stating that 'We need to recognize the *"name-of-the father"* as the foundation of the symbolic function' (Lacan 1966a : 278, our translation).

The basic idea is rather simple but far-reaching both in psychological and communicational terms. The link between child and mother is immediate, physical and concrete. The link is far more abstract between a child and its father, the man who calls it 'son' or 'daughter' and provides it with his name. This link is based on belief, on trust; it cannot be proven, modern molecular genetics apart. Only by accepting this link and accepting the father's name does the child fully enter into the realm of symbols and language with the severance of the immediate connection, both unsettling and endlessly fascinating, between words and the things they are meant to designate. Without this fundamental experience of receiving a 'name-of-the-father', which, by the way, is always validated by the mother, a truly symbolic signification cannot be formulated. One can think of this as if the relationship between a child and its father is in itself a symbolic relationship, the first symbolic relationship that will enable all others that follow.

The term 'symbolic signification' is used here in the wide sense of a form of communication that acknowledges the possibility of differences between a physical sign (a written or spoken word, an image, a symbol …), a personal mental image (a semantic entity, an idea, a concept …) and the real-world object it refers to. There are thus gaps between words and their meaning, as well as between the meaning of words and the real-world objects they refer to. The links between the three sub-codes are never entirely fixed or closed. Symbols are characterised by a degree of openness that can only be settled by way of an active investment that involves the use of personal experience, collective history and general context.

The inability of the Smithian individual in *The Theory of Moral Sentiments* to experience a convergence of the proliferating series of designations towards a single 'name' of the impartial spectator indicates the absence of a foundation for symbolic signification. The rapid and repeated enumeration of a series of qualities indicating authority, omniscience, ubiquity etc. is not sufficient for establishing a semantic entity sufficiently coherent and stable to allow for a mode of signification that can work with a gap between representation and the underlying meaning that is represented.

In the context of Adam Smith's work, we are primarily interested in the manner in which an individual deals with the gap between his outward appearance that is a building block of the sympathy mechanism and his 'true' feelings, as well as the gap between an object identified as a valuable good and its 'true' value, or, in other words, the gap between exchange value and use value. However, in the absence of a sufficiently strong anchor of the semantic system in form of the name of the impartial spectator, and hence in the absence of any such symbolic signification, the Smithian individual returns to the only mode of communication that is open to him, the identity of appearance and underlying reality, the iconic mode of signification. As discussed above, only the prevalence of such iconic signification as the basis for communication can provide the necessary conditions for a market economy. A corollary of such iconic signification is, of course, that exchange value must dominate use value.

Another clarification is in order here. When discussing the informational structures of Adam Smith's work, one needs to distinguish clearly between the author himself and the subject of his inquiries we call the 'Smithian individual'. It is only this individual who, in the exchanges with his peers, is limited to an iconic form of signification that is so beneficial for the construction of competitive markets. Adam Smith, the author, instead is a great, if eclectic, stylist who disposes of a broad range of rhetorical means reaching from dry logical deduction to the invocation of literary, philosophical or historical background information, all ingredients for allowing symbolic signification to function.

And yet, even at the level of the text itself, the two modes of signification are not equivalent or exchangeable in *The Theory of Moral Sentiments.* Each one is clearly associated with either the 'horizontal' or the 'vertical' axis in Adam Smith's work. When talking about the sympathy mechanism, Smith provides simple straightforward definitions, concluding with an iconic form of signification – things are what they seem for all to see. When presenting the impartial spectator instead, virtuous behaviour is suggested by historical example or inner voice. It is the weakness of this latter form of communication, evidenced by the absence of the 'moral sense' necessary for sustaining the interior dialogue with the impartial spectator, that will ultimately let the sympathy mechanism reign supreme towards the end of the book (see below). And without an appropriate form of communication, the vertical axis will not be sufficiently suggestive and be reduced to a drab exhortation to be virtuous. While the possibility that an appropriate 'name-of-the-father' can be found is not excluded, in the end a dominant doubt persists as to whether he could constitute a sufficiently solid anchor for a more open semantic universe, alternative to the conventional values provided by the sympathy mechanism.

The uncertainty surrounding the capacity of the impartial spectator to maintain a sufficiently convincing form of interaction with the Smithian individual contrasts with the fluid coherence and clarity of the presentation regarding the sympathy mechanism, whose capability to establish binding behavioural norms is never once put in doubt. The solid iconic signification it generates can be carried over without any loss to *The Wealth of Nations*, a book that no longer bears any direct traces of a need for more complete orientation – except in the very few passages already alluded to. In fact, towards the end of *The Theory of Moral Sentiments,* Adam Smith proceeds to a sort of rhetorical rejection of the impartial spectator as far as his direct and personal implication in the establishment of behavioural norms is concerned.

And yet, the triumph of the sympathy mechanism over the impartial spectator at the level of their direct confrontation does not end the fundamental tension between the two forces structuring Adam's Smith's work. First, the notion of justice associated with the impartial spectator remains an indispensable normative reference. More importantly, the tension is displaced. The victorious principle, the horizontal normativity of the sympathy mechanism, will be at the service of the defeated principle, the vertical normativity of the impartial spectator. The pursuit of a socially codified self-interest will be the most efficient means to realise the noble aspiration of general welfare. In this indirect manner, the heritage of the impartial spectator, the ethical objective of general welfare, is better preserved and accomplished by the market system built on the sympathy mechanism than through any direct intervention (see Chapter 4 'The paradoxical synthesis').

However, before one can demonstrate his survival or rather his resurrection in a new role, one will need to observe towards the end of *The Theory of Moral Sentiments* the definitive denial of the impartial spectator's ability to serve as a direct normative reference for human behaviour. This denial is enacted through Smith's explicit and comprehensively motivated refusal to accept the principal means of communication of the impartial spectator, personal introspection and interior dialogue. The fact that this refusal takes place while discussing the work of Frances Hutcheson, Adam Smith's professor and predecessor on the Chair of moral philosophy at the University of Glasgow and thus in some ways a father figure himself, provides added poignancy. This unique passage demonstrates once more a sophisticated interweaving of content and form typical for the author of *The World of Nations.*[6]

Criticism and refutation of the vertical principle

The continuous conflict between the two structuring forces – virtue according to the commandments of the impartial spectator and intersubjective sympathy in the context of personal wealth acquisition – comes to an abrupt conclusion at the end of *The Theory of Moral Sentiments.* This conclusion prepares the transition towards *The Wealth of Nations.* The high point of the conflict and its sudden end is played out in a lengthy discussion of the works of Frances Hutcheson that is composed of two parts, a eulogising introduction first and a violent refutation, second. Both parts are distinguished from the rest of the book by a particularly emphatic style.

The question at hand is the existence of a 'moral sense', a sort of inner voice permitting each individual to know instantaneously and with precision what is right and what is wrong with respect to questions of virtue. In his *Inquiry Concerning Virtue*, Hutcheson maintained that the ability to identify true virtue is based neither on reason nor self-interest but on this innate 'moral sense'. Adam Smith writes even of the moral sense as being '… somewhat analogous to the external senses' (Smith 1759 (VII.III.3.5): 379). Such an instinctive recognition of virtuous behaviour is also the hallmark of the interior dialogue with the impartial spectator which, strictly speaking, is not a dialogue but a one-way communication from the impartial spectator to the individual. It needs to be contrasted with the *rational* recognition of moral rules based on social conventions. At the beginning of the discussion, Adam Smith takes sides *in favour* of Hutcheson's work on the formation of formal judgement in the clearest terms:

> Dr Hutcheson had the merit of being the first who distinguished with any degree of precision in what respect all moral distinctions

> may be said to arise of reason, and in what respect they are founded upon immediate sense and feeling. In his illustrations upon the moral sense he has explained this so fully, and, in my opinion, so unanswerably, that, if any controversy is still kept about this subject, I can impute it to nothing, but either to inattention to what that gentleman has written, or to a superstitious attachment to certain forms of expression, a weakness not very uncommon among the learned, especially in subjects so deeply interesting as the present, in which a man of virtue is often loath to abandon, even the propriety of a single phrase which he has been accustomed to.
>
> (Smith 1759 (VII.III.2.9): 378)

The rhetorical force of this hyperbolic eulogy of Hutcheson and his theory of an immediate and instinctive moral sense is somewhat surprising given that a little earlier Smith still had remarked that:

> The general maxims of morality are formed, like all other general maxims, from experience and induction. We observe in a great variety of cases what pleases or displeases our moral faculties … and by induction from this experience, we establish those general rules.
>
> (Smith 1759 (VII.III.2.6): 377)

This statement is, in fact, more in tune with the form of preference formation generally advanced by Adam Smith.[7] Even though he admits the existence of a 'moral faculty', this faculty is not an absolute organ 'analogous to the external senses' but an ability to form a rational judgement on the basis of observation and induction. Smith insists, by the way, on the fact that induction is always operated by reason. Observation and induction are, of course, also the modus operandi of the sympathy mechanism. At the beginning of the discussion, however, Adam Smith limits this process to self-observation rather than to sympathetic mutual observation.

Nevertheless, the process described already makes it possible to relativise any moral norms whose primary criteria for acceptance are whether they 'please' one's moral faculty or not. One is far from the absolutism associated with the 'immediate sense and feeling' proffered by Hutcheson. Thus a latent conflict between two views on the issue can already be discerned in these introductory pages, even if Adam Smith at this point clearly is still eager to find a compromise allowing the accommodation of both the inductive action of reason and Hutcheson's moral sense:

> But though reason is undoubtedly the source of the general rules of morality … it is altogether absurd and unintelligible to suppose that the first perceptions of right and wrong can be derived from reason, even in those particular cases upon the experience of which the general rules are formed. These first perceptions, as well as all other experiments upon which any general rules are founded, cannot be the object of reason, but of immediate sense and feeling.
>
> (Smith 1759 (VII.III.2.7): 377)

However, this valiant attempt at reconciling the opposition between an absolute form of morality guaranteed by an external authority and a worldlier notion of morality depending on personal reasoning can only retard, but not avoid, the break-out of open conflict. Several pages later, Adam Smith begins with the definitive deconstruction of the notion of 'moral sense' and the idea of an autonomous source of behavioural norms that comes with it:

> But notwithstanding all the pains which this ingenious philosopher [Hutcheson] has taken to prove that the principle of approbation [the moral sense] is founded in a peculiar power of perception, somewhat analogous to the external senses, there are some consequences, which he acknowledges to follow from this doctrine that will, perhaps, be regarded by many as a sufficient confutation of it. The qualities, he allows, which belong to the objects of any sense, cannot, without the greatest absurdity, be ascribed to the sense itself.
>
> (Smith 1759 (VII.III.3.8): 381)

In the following, Adam Smith increasingly argues in favour of a formation of moral rules through an inter-subjective process based on reciprocal observation among peers. It is now the coincidence of the moral sentiments of the various members of a group of peers that becomes the essential criterion for accepting a moral rule. In fact, Smith now transposes the sympathy mechanism into the moral sphere without yet naming it. In parallel, he begins criticising Hutcheson's idea of a 'sense' for perceiving the morality of an action independently from social approbation.

> It must be said, that when the approbation with which our neighbour regards the conduct of a third person coincides with our own, we approve of his approbation, and consider it as, in some measure, morally good … It must be allowed, therefore, that … the coincidence or opposition of sentiments, between the observer and the person observed, constitutes moral approbation or disapprobation … Or to what purpose imagine a new power of perception in order to account for those sentiments?
>
> (Smith 1759 (VII.III.3.14): 384)

Adam Smith does not restrict himself to affirming his differences with his former tutor, but pushes the conflict to its limit. In the conclusion of his dissertation on the formation of moral rules, his argumentation has the clarity of a prosecutor's statement and his style the tone of an aggressive mockery. We are far indeed from the flattering eulogy of the introduction. This conclusion also reconnects the formation of moral rules explicitly with the sympathy mechanism. Of Hutcheson's 'moral sense' remains only a tiny 'overplus' that remains undefined:

> When we approve of any character or action, the sentiments which we feel, are, according to the foregoing system, derived from four sources … First, we sympathize with the motives of the agent; secondly, we enter into the gratitude of those who receive the benefit of his actions; thirdly, we observe that his conduct has been agreeable to the general rules by which those two sympathies generally act; and, last of all, when we consider such actions as making part of a system of behaviour which tends to promote the happiness either of the individual or of the society … After deducting, in any one particular case, all that must be acknowledged to proceed from some one or other of these four principles, I should be glad to know what remains, and I shall freely allow this overplus to be ascribed to a moral sense, or any other peculiar faculty, provided anybody will ascertain precisely what this overplus is.
>
> (Smith 1759 (VII.III.3.16): 385–86)

There are thus four routes by which moral rules can be established. The first three are based on sympathy: the first on direct sympathy, the second on indirect sympathy by way of gratitude and the third on the sympathy with the rules derived from the former two. The fourth route is the aesthetic pleasure derived from observing a certain action working in harmony with other such actions to a beneficial end. Smith compares it to the 'beauty … which we ascribe to any well-contrived machine' (ibid.). Each of these routes is capable, on its own, to lead towards the establishment of a moral rule and consequently Hutcheson's 'moral sense' no longer has a role to play. In the unlikely case there existed a gap (an 'overplus') between the whole of moral rules and the explanatory power of the four routes evoked, Smith is willing, in principle, to ascribe it to an autonomous entity capable of generating moral norms such as the 'moral sense'. However, even in this case, Smith sardonically concludes he would be glad to know of what this 'overplus' consisted. In other words, given that moral rules can be established entirely through interpersonal sympathy relations, there are simply no moral rules left out there, whose origins need explaining.

The above passage in Part VII at the end of *The Theory of Moral Sentiments* plays a crucial role in Adam Smith's work and opens the transition towards *The Wealth of Nations.* It marks the end of the direct dichotomy between the vertical principle of the 'impartial spectator' and the horizontal principle of the sympathy mechanism, but also prepares the indirect synthesis between the two (see Chapter 4 'The paradoxical synthesis'). The deconstruction of Hutcheson's approach signals, in fact, the end of the vertical principle as a direct reference for human action.

The moral sense, the immediate, physically palpable, reaction to the morality of a given action was the principal means of interior communication with the impartial spectator. Private deliberation, listening to the 'great inmate', was the only way to break the routine of sideways glances beckoning for sympathy. Once the principal mode of communication with the impartial spectator has been rejected, he loses his significance and cedes to the predominance of the horizontal principle inasmuch as the direct (or local) determination of human actions is concerned. As often, the style, manner and presentation of Adam Smith's discourse support and reinforce the content. The negation of the vertical principle is staged in form of the rejection of the theory of his former professor and predecessor Francis Hutcheson. Bereft of the 'moral sense', the impartial spectator will withdraw as far as the direct determination of human affairs is concerned.

Of course, the vertical axis will not disappear but will only depart from the front of the scene. As discussed, respect for all written law remains an indispensable prerequisite for any form of society, even after the Law of the impartial spectator is no longer operative. Even more importantly, we will see in the discussion of the 'invisible hand' in Chapter 4 that the Director of nature has withdrawn from direct interference in the affairs of the world only to let the mechanics of auto-organisation accomplish his own designs more efficiently. In the end, he himself created man in a manner that makes him more attuned to the opinions of his brethren than to the indications of the man within.

Nevertheless, these qualifications, even if important, should not obscure the fact that following the refusal of Hutcheson's moral sense, there is no longer a place in Adam Smith's work for an independent entity – moral, psychological or religious – that could pretend to the authority of directly determining human behaviour. From now on, humans will auto-organise themselves in a mechanism of social mimicry without being disturbed by ethical injunctions external to their own system. For the time being, it is of limited importance that the structure and finality of this process of auto-determination have been consciously conceived by a superior force. Henceforth, the specific appearance of the world will be shaped by humans for humans. At the end of *The Theory of Moral Sentiments*, the way is free for the great panorama of this world in *The Wealth of Nations*.

3.2 The economic passion

Passions and interests

The preceding sections presented and analysed the two normative frameworks that can generate rules and thus structure human behaviour for Adam Smith – the sympathy mechanisms and the impartial spectator. It is now possible to take an additional step in the understanding of the teleology of the social system conceived by Adam Smith. Both, the horizontal framework structured by the sympathy mechanism and the vertical framework structured by the impartial spectator have the power to control destructive and socially harmful passions or impulses. Both normative frameworks, however, also *use* the force of the passions, a force that will necessarily need to be tamed and canalised, to advance general welfare. This leaves the passions with a very ambivalent role. In their original form, they are harmful to social life and must thus be suppressed. On the other hand, they are indirectly the very foundation of sociability. This holds, in particular, for the strongest of the passions, the desire to be loved.

This section will attempt to analyse this double role of the passions in two steps. We will begin by presenting the recent discussion on the role of the passions in the work of Adam Smith. In a next step we will show, on the basis of a close reading of the original text, how Smith approached the problem himself. The solution to the problem of the double nature of the passions, the intricate interaction between the horizontal and the vertical framework, will be presented in Chapter 4.

The development of the role of the passions in Adam Smith's work is necessarily part of the discussion about the opposition between passions and interests in the eighteenth century. Albert Otto Hirschman, in particular, has introduced economists and historians of economic thought to this discussion in *The Passions and the Interests: Political Arguments for Capitalism before its Triumph*. It is useful to begin this description of the background with a brief presentation of the main thesis of this book and its commentary on the work of Adam Smith. According to Hirschman, the reign of human passions and their negative impact on social life has been a major issue of debate since the dawn of humanity. Poets, philosophers and political commentators have proposed, at various times, different solutions to the question. Among these solutions, Hirschman concentrates himself on a concept that he calls the principle of the 'compensating passion'. He identifies in the works of thinkers as diverse as Bacon, Spinoza, Hume, Vauvenargues and d'Holbach the idea that only the passions themselves can control the dangerous passions (Hirschman 1997: 20–31). Among others, Hirschman cites Spinoza saying that 'an affect cannot be restrained or removed unless by an opposed and stronger affect' and Vauvenargues for whom 'passions are opposed to passions and one can serve as a counterweight to another' (Hirschman 1997: 23 and 27).

Hirschman further develops this idea of an equilibrium of the passions in the context of a reading of the great political and historical commentators of the sixteenth to the eighteenth century such as La Rochefoucault, Montesquieu or Helvetius. His reasoning finally identifies a passion 'hitherto known as greed, avarice or love of lucre' that progressively balances and even dominates all other passions. From this idea arises, according to Hirschman, the concept of economic interest which will become synonymous with 'the innocence and sweetness of commerce'. The birth of this new notion of economic interest becomes, in turn, the foundation of a new theoretical endeavour as 'the development of economic theory depends on its autonomy or its specialisation and the separation of passions and interests' (Larrère 1999: 2, our translation).

In the context of the notion of an equilibrium of the passions, Hirschman sees economic interest as devoid of the destructive charge of the passions but still imbued with their dynamism. This idea is very useful also for understanding Adam Smith, who, in fact, presents an elaborate and highly personal version of this equilibrium of the passions. Under the influence of the sympathy mechanism, the destructive and socially harmful passions indeed transform themselves in *The Theory of Moral Sentiments* into a highly codified self-interest. This self-interest is, however, not a proper passion. It is rather the result of the equilibrium of the violent and disagreeable passions and the strongest of them all, the desire to be socially accepted, to be loved:

> Nature, when she formed man for society, endowed him with an original desire to please, and an original aversion to offend his brethren. She taught him to feel pleasure in their favourable, and pain in their unfavourable regard. She rendered their approbation most flattering and most agreeable to him for its own sake; and their disapprobation most mortifying and most offensive.
>
> (Smith 1759 (III.2.6): 135)

It is therefore surprising that Hirschman, after introducing the notion of an equilibrium of the passions, so useful for understanding Adam Smith, attacks him for having confused everything. According to Hirschman, Smith never properly distinguished between passions and economic interest – a rather surprising reproach considering the evident difference in this regard between *The Theory of Moral Sentiments* and *The Wealth of Nations.* The result is supposedly a one-dimensional vision of human behaviour, where all motives (whether based on passions or interests) are indiscriminately directed towards wealth accumulation:

> By holding that ambition, the lust for power, and the desire for respect can all be satisfied by economic improvement, Smith undercut the idea that passion can be pitted against passion, or the interests against the passions. This whole train of thought becomes suddenly incomprehensible, if not nonsensical, and there is a return to the stage, prior to Bacon, when the major passions were considered a solid bloc and to feed on each other.
>
> (Hirschman 1997: 110)

Or,

> Adam Smith abandoned the distinction between the interests and the passions in making his case for the unfettered pursuit of private gain.
>
> (Hirschman 1997: 69)

Hirschman attempts to corroborate his idea by citing a short passage from the fourth book of *The Wealth of Nations* in which Smith comments on the advancement of the economy by individuals who are moved by 'private interests and passions' (Smith 1776 (IV.7.3): 652). This approach is very partial indeed. In *The Wealth of Nations*, Smith considered the problem of the violent and original passion as largely solved. The very notion of a 'passion' is thus no longer the same as in *The Theory of Moral Sentiments* and one is rather confronted with a derived or secondary passion akin to a sentiment. That said, Adam Smith no longer uses either term very often in *The Wealth of Nations*. In *The Theory of Moral Sentiments* instead, the conflict between primary and secondary passions, or between passions and sentiments, is still very much alive. The whole perspective of the book is defined by the question of how to channel the socially destructive primary passions by converting them into socially acceptable self-interest.

Adam Smith's deliberation turns around the question of 'self-command' and the conditions under which it is able to control the passions, frequently characterised as childish, for the benefit of the individual and society. Of course, self-command can be motivated either by the desire for sympathy, or the respect for the impartial spectator. Either way, it assumes *the* key role in this context and is the very thing of which virtue is made: 'Self-command is not only itself a great virtue, but from it, all the other virtues seem to derive their principal lustre' (Smith 1759 (VI.III.11): 284). The most dangerous of the passions, those that need to be controlled most urgently, are anger and resentment. The section 'Of the unsocial passions' begins with the words:

> There is another set of passions, which, though derived from the imagination, yet before we can enter into them, or regard them as graceful or becoming, must always be brought down to a pitch much lower than to which undisciplined nature would raise them. These are, hatred and resentment, with all their different modifications … Their immediate effects are so disagreeable, that even if they are most justly provoked, there is still something about them which disgusts us.
>
> (Smith 1759 (I.II.3.1–5 p. 41–44)

Self-control and the moderation of emotions, which constitutes the essence of the sympathy mechanism, needs to begin at a very early age, as soon as the individual begins to socialise outside of the family. The sympathy mechanism literally begins in the school yard:

> A very young child has no self-command; but, whatever are its emotions, whether fear or grief, or anger, it endeavours always, by the violence of its outcries, to alarm, as much as it can, the attention of its nurse, or of its parents … When it is old enough to go to school, or to mix with its equals, it soon finds that they have no such indulgent partiality. It naturally wishes to gain their favour, and to avoid their hatred or contempt. Regard even to its own safety teaches it to do so; and it soon finds that it can do so in no other way than by moderating, not only its anger, but all its other passions, to the degree which its play-fellows and companions are likely to be pleased with. It thus enters into the great school of self-command …
>
> (Smith 1759 (III.3.22): 167)

The control of the passions is the essential prerequisite for participation in the sympathy mechanism and, beyond, for any form of economic behaviour, that is behaviour defined by a carefully controlled self-interest on the basis of socially codified preferences, as has been developed above.

In developing his reasoning, Adam Smith places himself, despite the originality of his final construction, fully in the midst of the discussion by the thinkers of the Scottish Enlightenment of the conditions for sociability. The opposite would have been surprising, as both, his professor, Francis Hutcheson, as well as his older friend and mentor, David Hume, were eminent contributors to this discussion. While Smith is at the origin of the definitive emancipation of economics from political or social considerations, the roots and defining questions of his work are firmly set in a well-established philosophical and political tradition. It is Hirschman's great merit, having brought out the central faultline of this tradition and having demonstrated its fertility to economists. However, his wish to exclude Adam Smith from this tradition is curious, to say the least.

In the past, Jean-Pierre Dupuy had already taken up a position against Hirschman's remarks. Dupuy, in particular, took issue with Hirschman's separation of 'economic interests' from 'passions' which he considered far too neat.[8] In his interpretation of Adam Smith, Dupuy is, ironically, relatively close to Hirschman, as both imply that Smith did *not* make a clear distinction between interest and passions. For Hirschman this is a regrettable sign of regression given the state of the contemporary discussion; for Dupuy it is a considerable advance. For the Adam Smith of Jean-Pierre Dupuy, economic interest remains rooted in the passions: 'the interests are contaminated … Smith knows that the interests contain the passions in the sense that they are infected' (Dupuy 1988: 84, our translation). In his following book, Dupuy specifies that 'sympathy contains envy, in the two senses of the word contain' and 'he [Smith] knows full well that self-love is essentially the result of being recognised by others and that the search for material gain … creates between them passionate relationships' (Dupuy 1992: 100, our translation).

For all its perspicacity and rhetorical elegance, Dupuy's idea of an Adam Smith, advocate of a passionate economic interest, needs to be firmly qualified. Dupuy is right to underline the origin of economic interest in the passions and the 'residue' of passion in economic relations. His argument puts Smith once more squarely at the centre of the debate about the compensating passions. However, one must not forget that this does not create a simple blend between passions on the one hand and interests on the other. The two are manifestations of human motives at different levels of socialisation. Economic interests on their own are a thoroughly transformed and socialised manifestation of the passions. They are 'lopped and bound', to use Mandeville's words, not only by justice but also by a desire for social recognition that will not be satisfied without substantial and continuous self-control.

At the concrete level of everyday social interaction, passions and interests are characterised for Adam Smith by a radical opposition, whatever the subterranean interrelations of their respective origins. For Smith, open manifestations of passion destroy the social tissue, while the exercise of economic interest is essential for weaving it. Not insisting time and again on this distinction risks comforting Hirschman's absurd point of view that a negligent Adam Smith confounds passions and interests due to insouciance and ideological partisanship in favour of the profit motive. When he does not write about Adam Smith, who seems to inspire in him a particularly ungenerous reading, Hirschman takes a differentiated approach to the interaction between passions and reason that is close to the final Smithian synthesis:

> Once passion was deemed destructive and reason ineffectual … A reason of hope was therefore conveyed by the wedging of interest in between the two traditional categories of human motivation. Interest was seen to partake in effect of the better nature of each,

> as the passion of self-love upgraded and contained by reason, and as reason given direction and force by that passion.
>
> (Hirschman 1997: 44)

The author of *The Theory of Moral Sentiments* himself would not have repudiated such a statement.

In order to do full justice to the role that passions and interests play in Smith's work, both as far as their different social functions and their partial consubstantiality are concerned, one needs to insist on the *transformation* of the passions. We have already seen in Chapter 2 that the competition for social recognition by one's peers was transformed, under the codifying force of the sympathy mechanism, into 'emulation', a form of competition in likeness, and ultimately a quest for wealth accumulation.

The sympathy mechanism indeed plays a key role in the process of transforming the passions into interests without abolishing them as such. The passions constitute the material from which the interests are created. One could also say that the interests represent a socially acceptable and beneficial expression of the original passions. The expression of 'contamination' that Jean-Pierre Dupuy uses, renders well the indestructible link between passions and interests but does not inform us about the precise nature of the transformation that precedes this residual contamination. This transformation consists of two elements, moderation and codification. First, the passions need to be brought down from a level that constitutes a physical danger to others; second, they need to find expressions that are comprehensible to all and can be inserted into a social context. These socially compatible expressions of the passions are the interests. The questions of the relations between passions and interests thus cannot be reduced to a simple question of opposition or identity.

Despite the difference in historical period, the modern psychoanalytic notions of 'repression' and 'displacement' cover perfectly well the mechanism implied by Adam Smith. The economic interests are, in fact, the displaced and socially positive manifestations of the repressed passions or impulses. In their original and unaltered state, they were highly detrimental to social life. Smith himself insists several times – most remarkably in the passages concerning the 'invisible hand' – that this beneficial displacement of the repressed passions into the economic domain takes place *unconsciously*.

However, when using the terms 'repression' and 'displacement', which carry their own semantic baggage, care needs to be taken not to import too hastily related psychoanalytic notions into the discussion.

For instance, the cause that triggers repression of the impulses in Freudian psychoanalysis is the fear of castration. The repression of the original passions in *The Theory of Moral Sentiments,* instead, is set off by the fear of social ostracism or, in Smith's words, 'mortifying disapprobation'.

Adam Smith's position regarding the passions is thus of a very precise ambivalence. This ambivalence is revealed in an exemplary manner in his investigation of physical violence. Smith's attitude towards physical violence differs completely, depending on whether he discusses spontaneous individual violence, the result of a badly controlled impulse, or political and social violence that is organised and codified. We know that he rejects the first form of violence without any concessions. It is the function of justice to control, suppress and punish it. His attitude towards forms of physical violence having a social function is, however, completely different. Smith evokes such cases with detached neutrality. In examples as different as the one of a soldier, who equates his pay to the probability of dying in the field, or of the colonial empires of Latin America, which have seen substantial population growth despite the massacres perpetrated against the indigenous Indians, individual human life does not constitute an absolute value for Adam Smith. Naturally, he always talks approvingly of any form of legal violence in the pursuit of justice, capital punishment included.

This apparent contradiction is explained by the fact that, for Adam Smith, the supreme value is *not* individual happiness or the protection of the individual but the preservation of the group, the family, the nation or the country. For Smith, individual violence constitutes a threat to society; socially organised violence structures it. Not grasping this distinction is an endless source of misunderstanding, due to which critics ascribe all sorts of shortcomings and contradictions to Smith. Of course, Smith's lasting contribution remains the insight that allowing and furthering the pursuit of individual self-interest is, ultimately, also the most efficient means for preserving and furthering general social welfare. However, this is the result of a painstaking inquiry into the sources of durable sociability. Knut Haakonssen, for instance, cites Smith with the words that '… the continued stability of the society … [is] the most urgent "public utility"' (Haakonssen 1998: 168). Considering his economic liberalism as an ideological position taken *ex ante*, as Hirschman does, for example, means barring oneself from understanding the key impetus of his work.

Socially codified violence exercised by the state needs to serve a carefully considered purpose. It receives its justification from containing anarchic individual violence and thus stabilising society. This social control of individual impulses remains, of course, a necessary precondition for any form of exchange or of the division of labour. The contradiction concerning the Smithian position towards violence is thus only apparent and vanishes once one accepts that the survival and the prosperity of the group are the final objectives of Adam Smith's teleology. Economic individualism contributes to these objectives in an essential manner and thus attains a nobleness of purpose that was not part of its original intention (see also Chapter 4 'The paradoxical synthesis').

Self-control and the society of 'brothers'

The Smithian figure of a suppression of violent, individual passions by means of organised and codified violence in order to create the basis for social life, finds its echo more than a century later in Sigmund Freud's famous essay about the origins of human society *Totem and Taboo*. The structural similarities between their respective arguments allow further deepening of our understanding of the role of the passions in Adam Smith's work. The principal analogy between *Totem and Taboo* and *The Theory of Moral Sentiments* consists in the fact that in both cases individual anarchic violence is contained by the establishment of a homogeneous, egalitarian society based on contract and the observance of law. The similarities between the two authors can be surprising, as, for instance, when Freud describes the evolution of a society of peers ('brothers' in the Freudian terminology) structured by economic exchange once the individual passions or impulses have been domesticated.

In Freud's work, the founding act for this new civilisation is the elimination of the brutal primal father who reigns with absolute power over the primal horde (Freud 1997: 410–412). Once the 'brothers' have banded together to murder the primal father, the fear for their own lives in a deadly chaos pushes them to organise themselves under the sign of renouncing the pursuit of their impulses. This concerns, primarily, the famous three fundamental interdictions of cannibalism, murder and incest (and, more widely, unstructured sexual relations). Peaceful exchange, contract and the respect of the written law are now substituted for autocratic domination and now become, according to Freud, the new foundations of society:

> The social and fraternal feelings that are responsible for this great revolution maintain now, and for long-time, the most profound

> influence over the development of society … Safeguarding each other's life, the brothers stipulate that no one amongst them has the right to be treated by the others as the father has been treated by all of them together. Thus they exclude a repetition of the father's fate.
>
> (Freud 1997: 429)

The motivation behind this new form of self-control is fear of a return of violence. Each brother fears nothing more than the return of the dead father. This fear is all the more present since assuming the dead father's position and becoming the new absolute father of the horde is, of course, the most ardent and absolutely inadmissible wish of each and every one of them.

Justice and contract thus become, according to Freud, the indispensable pillars of this new egalitarian society. Part of this new social infrastructure will be religion, which will allow appeasement of the sense of guilt, and the achievement of a certain form of reconciliation with the father. The passions are thus contained, controlled and can be converted into more or less peaceful interests. With Freud as with Smith, the interests in their new form remain coloured, or 'contaminated', by the original impulses. All through his long essay – and throughout his work, as we know – Freud insists on the subterranean survival of the suppressed passions that gives life in society its peculiar flavour, constituted by a mix of renouncement and uneasy accommodation.

This is because the effort of containment and transformation of the original impulses is not without cost. In particular, this new society is characterised by a profound sadness, or, more precisely, melancholy. This melancholy is nourished both by grieving for the dead father and the frustration of being unable to assume his position and to liberate the original impulses. Again, we find precisely the same motive in *The Theory of Moral Sentiments.* Shortly before the elimination of the impartial spectator during the course of the rejection of Hutcheson's moral sense, Smith writes:

> To … universal benevolence, on the contrary, the very suspicion of a fatherless world, must be the most melancholy of all reflections …
>
> (Smith 1759 (VI.II.3.2): 277)

It is significant that Smith associates this emotion with the practice of benevolence. Benevolence, we recall, was one of the virtues closely associated with the impartial spectator. It is only in this vertical dimension that the melancholy over an absent father can be experienced. The same experience is meaningless in a horizontal dimension organised by the sympathy mechanism, whose very existence is conditional on the absence of a father figure or any other autonomous authority. Of course, the defining characteristic of the world presented by Adam Smith remains the fact that the 'local' elimination of the impartial spectator will facilitate attaining his final objectives at a general level (see Chapter 4). This is Adam Smith's most original and optimistic contribution, which clearly distinguishes him also from writers such as Freud. In Freud's works, the legacy of the slain primal father lives on in an unmitigated discontent with civilisation but without the productive energy to achieve any ulterior, great design.

Nevertheless, the basic structure of the argument of both writers remains the same: to motivate, on the basis of psychological and anthropological determinants, the emergence of a society of equals based on exchange, contract and respect for the written law. In both cases, the repression and displacement of primary impulses is a cornerstone of this project. Both authors also put great store in the process of standardisation and codification of values, language and behaviour, behind which will always lurk the malleable but ultimately indestructible force of the passions. In Freud's case, this necessary step for any civilization is primarily interpreted as a cost and a source of suffering, for which only psychoanalytical therapy, and to some extent artistic sublimation, can provide remedy. In Smith's case, the same step is interpreted more positively as the basis for creating social advancement and economic behaviour, which sets in motion a process of auto-organisation between rational economic agents that has the most beneficial outcomes for society as a whole. This does not prevent Smith from also having the clearest view of the individual human costs of this process. In the horizontal society of peers, behaviour that is exclusively formatted by social expectation and sympathy will always be 'second best'.

Once the psychological bases have been defined, *The Wealth of Nations* provides the imposing canvas of the process of auto-organisation that has thus been set in motion. One should never forget, however, the conditions necessary for its functioning, which are the homogenisation of preferences, the reduction of transaction costs and the progressive abolition of monopolies in a context in which the government limits itself essentially to defence and the administration of justice. *The Theory of Moral Sentiments* makes this vision possible by motivating these conditions. Their emergence is neither automatic nor costless. It is the result of a major conflict between two competing normative frameworks structured respectively by the impartial spectator and the sympathy mechanism. This conflict has far-reaching reverberations. It is also the conflict between two philosophical doctrines and of two different mental and informational structures, which lets us define this conflict as a struggle between an ethical and a moral orientation of the individual. The next section will explore the manner in which Adam Smith stages this conflict using his prodigious knowledge of philosophical, historical and literary references as well as of his talent for rhetorical exposition and dramatisation.

Ethics and morality

Following the injunctions of the impartial spectator leads to heroic anti-conformism guided by noble values but is also prone to cause haughty and antisocial individualism. Abandoning oneself to the sympathy mechanism and the shared, inter-subjective values that come with it would instead imply an easy sociability based on mutual emulation and generate a number of social benefits. This dichotomy is not unique to Adam Smith. It has been developed by several writers in terms of an opposition between 'ethics' and 'morality', which is eminently useful for further understanding the double system of co-ordinates that structures Smith's work. The vertical principle, defined by values structured around the impartial spectator, can thus be characterised as being at the origin of an *ethic* of timeless generality in its basic principles and perfectly individual in its concrete elaboration. The horizontal principle, structured by the sympathy mechanism, is, instead, at the origin of a socially sanctioned *morality* contingent on its historical and geographic context but unable to reflect this contingency in its formulation.

The French philosopher Norbert Waszek has shown convincingly that the origins of this opposition between a system of ideal, abstract norms and a system of socially defined practical norms in Adam Smith's work are rooted in Greek Stoic philosophy. In particular, he underlines the importance of the notions *katorthoma* and *kathekon* to understand the double nature of *The Theory of Moral Sentiments* (Waszek, 1984: 92–93). The first term, *katorthoma*, indicates an action in full coherence with the principles of Stoic philosophy, the first of which is self-control. The second term, *kathekon*, indicates a conventional action that is satisfactory from the point of view of established customs and requirements.

Waszek goes on to show that Smith develops this conflict between behaviour in perfect coherence with the impartial spectator and conventional behaviour explicitly, and at some length, in the long first chapter of the second section of book VII of *The Theory of Moral Sentiments*. Proceeding with the logic established with the elimination of Hutcheson's moral sense, Smith criticises any interpretation of Stoic principles overly attached to *katorthoma* as a pedantic aberration.[9] In the following, he proceeds with his own synthesis of Stoic philosophy that centres on the notion of 'practical morality':

> The Stoics in general seem to have admitted that there might be a degree of proficiency in those who had not advanced to perfect virtue and happiness. They distributed those proficient into different classes, according to the degree of their advancement; and they called the imperfect virtues which they supposed them capable of exercising, not rectitudes, but proprieties, fitnesses, decent and becoming actions, for which a plausible or probable reason could be assigned to what Cicero expresses by the Latin word officia, and Seneca, I think more exactly, by that of convenientia. The doctrine of those imperfect, but attainable virtues, seems to have constituted what we may call the practical morality of the Stoics.
>
> (Smith 1759 (VII.II.1.42): 344)

This is not the place to discuss the appropriateness of Smith's synthesis of Stoic philosophy based primarily on later Roman thinkers rather than their Greek predecessors. The interest of book VII in this context is how Smith employs the philosophical discussion to legitimise his own project. The 'imperfect but attainable virtues' identified in Stoic philosophy thus directly refer to the virtues he associates with the sympathy mechanism – prudence and propriety.

The age-old opposition between an ideal action, coherent with principles both abstract and intimate, on the one hand, and an appropriate and convenient action, coherent with social mores, on the other, has been taken up more recently by Henri Bergson and Paul Ricœur. Their work is of particular interest in this context as they cast this question in a dichotomy between ethics and morality, which not only reflects two equally valid normative references, but also refers to two diverse informational structures or tonalities that have different functions with respect to the construction and confirmation of a personal identity. This is what makes their contributions particularly fruitful for a better understanding of Adam Smith's work.

In *Soi-même comme un autre* (*Oneself as Another*, 1990), Paul Ricœur develops the origins of the notions of 'ethics' and 'morality'. Establishing that it is impossible to distinguish the two concepts on the basis of their etymology, one having a Greek, the other a Latin origin and both referring to a notion of customs or mores, he defines them as follows:

> I will reserve the term ethics for the impetus of an accomplished life and the term morality for the realisation of this impetus with the help of norms that pretend to be universal and that constitute constraints … One will easily recognise in the distinction between impetus and norm the opposition between two heritages, an Aristotelian heritage, where ethics are characterised by their teleological perspective, and a Kantian heritage, where morality is defined by the obligatory character of the norm and thus by a deontological viewpoint.
>
> (Ricœur 1990: 200, our translation)

When an individual attempts to identify directly with the objective of the impartial spectator in a teleological perspective, he strives to behave ethically. When he abides by the norms established by the sympathy mechanism, thus following a deontology, hoping that his actions will be irreproachable from the point of view of those around him, he obeys a morality. In his further development of this opposition, Ricœur formulates three principles. First, ethics comes before morality. Second, in practice, the ethical impetus must take the form of observable moral norms. Third, in case of conflict or contradiction, direct recourse to the ethical impetus is possible (ibid.).

The first two principles are expressed identically by Smith in the passages concerning the two tribunals. The tribunal of the impartial spectator that is interested in the extent to which the individual identifies with the *objectives* of the impartial spectator is higher in principle. In practice, however, it is the tribunal of men that is interested in the observation of behavioural norms by whom any action shall be judged. The relations with the third principle are more complex, partly because of the progression from *The Theory of Moral Sentiments* to *The Wealth of Nations*. In the latter, any action that has not been formatted by an established social morality is considered problematic. In *The Wealth of Nations*, strict observance of the social norm also inexorably fulfils the promise of the original impetus provided by the impartial spectator. There is thus no contradiction between a teleological and a deontological orientation and the problem of a conflict in the sense of Ricœur's third principle thus no longer exists in Smith's world.

But the distinction between ethics and morals intervenes not only, and perhaps not even primarily, at the level of verifiable practice but also at the level of their informational structure and emotional tonality. In *Les deux sources de la morale et de la religion* (*The Two Sources of Morality and Religion*, 1932, 1990), Henri Bergson enquires in particular about the emotional experiences associated with a 'closed morality' and an 'open morality'. The former is thus linked to a notion of pleasure or well-being and the latter to a notion of 'joy':

> Between the first morality [the one Ricœur calls 'morality'] and the second [the one Ricœur calls 'ethics'] thus lies all the distance that exists between rest and movement. The first is considered unchangeable. If it changes, it forgets immediately that it has changed or will not admit the change … The other however is a thrust, a need for movement; it is the very principle of movement … This establishes a difference in vital tone. He who regularly practices the morality of the city will experience that feeling of well-being which is common to the individual and to society and which results from the mutual interference of their material resistances. But the soul that opens itself and for whom the material obstacles vanish, belongs entirely to joy. Pleasure and well-being are something indeed; joy is more.
>
> (Bergson 1932: 56f, our translation)

With respect to Adam Smith's work, three points in the above passage merit our attention. First of all, we find the same attention paid to the tonality, the emotional atmosphere that Smith evokes in connection with 'second-best' behaviour exclusively structured by the desire to satisfy observable social norms. The courteous friend unable to feel true gratitude or the polite wife that has grown cold to her husband both act correctly from a deontological point of view (see above). Smith, however, is unequivocal about the fact that a vital element of human interaction is missing in their behaviour even though he insists that it cannot be enforced by any third party.

The second point of interest is that Bergson opposes a notion of well-being (*bien-être* in the French original) to a notion of 'joy'. While joy is difficult to define, a question we will come back to further below, it is quite obvious that well-being, the 'result of the mutual interference of their material resistances', is closely related to the notion of economic well-being or utility. This underlines the proximity of a notion of economic interest to the adoption of the values created by the sympathy mechanism, resulting in a closed form of morality. It also shows that it is inevitable that *The Theory of Moral Sentiments* advances to a social order structured by economic interest, once the possibility of an 'open morality' has been discarded together with the moral sense. The fact that this interest is referred to as 'self-interest' does not in the least diminish its firm anchoring in a closed, that is unalterable, set of *social* norms, from the point of view of the individual.

The third point concerns the discontinuous, diachronic and ahistorical character of the closed morality. The same quality was already observed in connection with the economic values shaped by the sympathy mechanism (see Part II above). An individual who receives his values exclusively from the auto-referential feedback loops of the sympathy mechanism or from the 'morality of the city' is devoid of any means to put these values in context or perspective. Of course, from a point of view external to the system, these values are perfectly arbitrary, as chance decides on the 'strange attractor' on which the opinions of different individuals converge. Such values will change with the whims of fashion but without ever reflecting such changes. From the point of view of an individual partaking in the process of social preference formation, they are indeed absolute and timeless. Were it to be otherwise, the very credibility of his participation in the process and the connected prize of social acceptability would be thrown into doubt. Bergson expresses this particular feature of the closed morality with the words that it does 'not admit', in fact cannot admit, any change.

Let us turn now towards the notion of an open morality that Bergson opposes to the closed morality that he associates with 'joy', and that Ricœur refers to as ethics. Most importantly, its definition is, each and every time, a particular operation which defines an individual's identity in relation to an authority that does not depend on the individual's actions. In the case of Adam Smith, this ethic is negotiated between the exacting demands of the impartial spectator and the thrust of a passion that is always and inevitably obstructed. Following an ethic implies a certain amount of self-consciousness about one's original passion to be loved, as well as an insight into the need for limits. Regarding the distinction between morals and ethics at the level of an individual's psychological structure, Gérard Pommier remarks:

> One must distinguish the ethical position from a moral commandment … At an unconscious level, the Law delimits an ethic that governs a subject's existence … The unconscious desire

> [that is associated with it] contradicts the moral rule of the brothers that rules social life.
>
> (Pommier 1996: 195–96, our translation)

The definition of a personal ethic is always the result of an open-ended, yet never arbitrary, search process. Its objective includes the aspiration of establishing a person's full identity with him- or herself. This is also the very corollary of joy. For Bergson, for instance, this ethical search can take the form of meditating the over-determined phrases of the gospels. For Smith, it renders a person capable of disinterested generosity towards others or the community. Of course, the concrete form of an individual's ethical position is never definitely formatted. The values elaborated in an interior dialogue with the impartial spectator, the gospels, or a heroic ambition to serve a higher ideal, are open by definition. They require constant interaction with a perpetually changing personal and historical context. If an ethical commitment could be fully codified, its observation would become the issue of a deontological obligation and it would lose its specific aspiration to follow the Law by the spirit rather than by the letter.

The opposition between morality and ethics is thus not only being played out at the level of content but also at the level of style and form. Adam Smith is no exception here. His discussion of ethical behaviour advances with the help of historical and literary examples that dramatise universal human conflicts (see the next sub-section for a number of particularly incisive examples). In other words, the elaboration of ethical struggles takes place by way of metaphorical or symbolic allusion rather than by the explicit presentation and subsequent logical deduction that characterise the passages about the sympathy mechanism. Bergson associates this difference in style and communicational mode with the fundamental structure of the human mind:

> … the first form of morality is relatively easy to formulate, but the second is not. Our intelligence and our language concentrate on things; they are much less at ease representing transitions or progress.
>
> (Bergson 1932: 57)

Morality, at least in the sense in which we use the term here following Ricœur, instead defines unequivocal rules of human behaviour when interacting with others. There exists no moral rule that can be formulated outside of this social space. In the case of Adam Smith, things are straightforward once the impartial spectator has been evicted together with the moral sense as a reference for any competing norm. The only remaining rules are those defined by the sympathy mechanism. They are automatically stabilised and enforced by the all-pervasive desire for social acceptance. In this perspective, the problem of the 'passions' is solved, since they have been permanently transformed into economic self-interest and an unflinching motivation to increase one's material wealth. At the level of individual behaviour, Dupuy is thus right to state that for Smith 'morals and economics are the object of one single and identical scientific discipline' (Dupuy 1992: 101, our translation).

This world, with its immanent morality, then works at the micro-level without any disturbing influence from the 'great judge and arbiter' and without any individual ethical search. As already mentioned, the vertical dimension retains its rights in terms of the final objective of the Smithian system, its teleology, which remains the general well-being of the nation. Also, one should not forget the notion of justice, whose original association with the Law of the impartial spectator is transformed into an unyielding respect for the written, human law. It has thus been 'orthogonalised', projected from the vertical into the horizontal dimension for daily, social use. The notion of justice thus continues to carry both moral and ethical elements.

A society without ethics is not a permissive society – quite to the contrary. The absence of the impartial spectator and hence the impossibility to stage the eternal drama between the forces of passion, the drama of their inevitable defeat and the possible redemption of the hero, demand an ever more efficient self-control. In order to appease the nagging feeling of doubt, the individual will be forced to align himself with ever- increasing zeal with the rules of the fraternal society. Abandoning his ethical project and the dialogue with the impartial spectator leaves no other option for satisfying the desire to be loved. The result is a permanent tension between a doubly frustrated passion and the hunger for a soothing social respectability. The frustrated passion is not only unable to realise itself, but its very existence and the history of its frustration are denied. The hunger for social respectability assumes the role of a palliative that requires it be taken in ever greater doses in order to remain effective. At the most fundamental level, the Smithian individual remains torn between the articulation of the passions in an ethical project and his desire for social acceptance in the moral terms stipulated by society. The result is, as we have seen, a profound melancholy.

Ethics and morality in the works and life of Adam Smith

Let us return to the study of the conflict between ethics and morality in the works of Adam Smith himself. For the greater part of *The Theory of Moral Sentiments*, an ethical orientation that receives its impetus from the impartial spectator and a moral orientation structured by the sympathy mechanism coexist, compete and complete each other. In the transition to *The Wealth of Nations*, this coexistence is progressively replaced by the exclusive importance of moral norms for determining the appropriateness of human behaviour.

The title of *The Theory of Moral Sentiments* seems to confirm such a predominance of morality over ethics, but one needs to remain prudent. The word 'moral' used by Adam Smith in the title and in the text can refer to both, a notion of morality and a notion of ethics. Quite frequently, however, what we would call ethical behaviour is indicated as 'virtuous' behaviour. The one time that Adam Smith mentions the term 'Ethics' explicitly, he uses it in precisely the same sense as later do Ricœur and Bergson, that is, in the sense of a personal and open normative framework. He compares its form, in fact, to literary criticism and opposes it to a closed and fully codified morality. In coherence with his earlier conclusions, its pursuit is a personal option rather than a social obligation:

> Such works [the *Ufficii* of Cicero or the *Ethics* of Aristotle] present us with agreeable and lively pictures of manners. By the vivacity of their descriptions they inflame our natural love of virtue and increase our abhorrence of vice: by the justness as well may often help both to correct and to ascertain our natural sentiments with regard to the propriety of conduct, and suggesting many nice and delicate attentions, form us to a more exact justness of behaviour, than what, without such instruction, we should have been apt to think of. In treating the rules of morality, in this manner, consists the science which is properly called Ethics, a science which, though like criticism it does not admit of the most accurate precision, is, however, both highly useful and agreeable.
>
> (Smith 1759 (VII.IV.6): 389)

We will see in the following that this passage also well describes Smith's own manner of communicating notions of ethical behaviour in *The Theory of Moral Sentiments.* Ethical behaviour is introduced without exception with the help of suggestive examples, frequently taken from ancient history, which may inflame the reader with a 'natural love of virtue'.

There clearly is a development between *The Theory of Moral Sentiments* and *The Wealth of Nations* at this level. In his first book, Adam Smith still maintains the option of ethical behaviour against the unconditional rule of a social morality conceived by the sympathy mechanism. In his second book, social morality rules untrammelled. We have shown in Chapter 2 of this book that this morality is arbitrary from a point of view *ex ante*. Any set of moral rules will do, given that its function is not to achieve any exogenously defined objective but to moderate and channel the destructive force of the passions and thus to enable social life as such. Its only purpose is to ensure the survival of the individual and of the group.

In *The Theory of Moral Sentiments,* unadulterated, natural sentiments can still dominate a relativism that knows no other absolute values than 'general welfare', even if already at this point the presentation of an ethical standpoint can be laced with irony (see below for examples). In *The Wealth of Nations*, however, there no longer exists any direct ethical position. Virtually any social custom that can be shown to play a stabilising role for the group is acceptable. The main criterion for social values is that they facilitate the game of intersubjective sympathy and wealth acquisition. All ethical projects or gratuitous gestures are now abandoned as potentially disturbing for the smooth running of the social machine.

The progression towards the total dominance of a paradigm, in which the final impact on the well-being of the collective is the exclusive criterion for judging an action, reveals itself in a particularly striking manner in the comparison of two passages, in which Adam Smith deals with the highly charged issue of infanticide. In the chapter programmatically called 'Of the Influence of Custom and Fashion upon Moral Sentiments' in *The Theory of Moral Sentiments*, Smith qualifies infanticide, while tolerated by the Greeks and other 'savage' nations, as 'a horrible abuse, [supported by] far-fetched considerations of public utility' and a 'dreadful violation of humanity'. Smith refutes the practice in the strongest terms even though he details the degree to which it was engrained in custom and socially widely approved:

> Uninterrupted custom had by this time so thoroughly authorised the practice that … even the doctrine of philosophers, which ought to have been more just and accurate, was led away by the established custom and upon this, as upon many other occasions,

> instead of censuring, supported the horrible abuse, by far-fetched considerations of public utility … There is an obvious reason why custom should never pervert our sentiments … There never can be any such custom. No society could subsist a moment, in which the usual strain of men's conduct and behaviour was of a piece with the horrible practice I have just now mentioned.
>
> (Smith 1759 (V.2.15–16): 246–47)

Very clearly, Smith develops a position in which an ethical standpoint dominates any moral conventions. Such principled opposition against established social mores associated with a 'perversion of the sentiments' no longer exists in *The Wealth of Nations*, where Smith precisely adopts the sort of relativistic reasoning he rejects in the passage cited above. Discussing a second time the issue of infanticide, this time in China, he frames the question exclusively in terms of social utility. The discussion concludes with the dispassionate observation that China has not regressed economically, that its cities have not been deserted and that agricultural land has not been abandoned (Smith 1776 (I.I.8): 81).

In principle, there is thus a stark contrast between Smith's position in *The Theory of Moral Sentiments* and *The Wealth of Nations*. However, a closer reading reveals the ambivalence of Smith's position already in the earlier work. In fact, the double discussion of the question of infanticide is an excellent example for showing how *The Wealth of Nations* continues and radicalises a type of reasoning that was already latent in *The Theory of Moral Sentiments* but constituted only one side of Smith's still evolving thought. While the passage in *The Theory of Moral Sentiments* clearly rejects infanticide as a 'dreadful violation of humanity', the same passage also prepares the later argumentation in terms of public utility. In fact, Smith solves the contradiction between a principles-based ethical approach ('infanticide is inhuman') and a custom-based social morality ('infanticide does not constitute a problem for social development') by saying that what *should not* be, *cannot* be. In a perfectly Darwinian logic, Smith argues that any society condoning infanticide would immediately put its own survival at grave risk. With the help of this somewhat sketchy argument – after all Smith had at length described the prevalence of the practice among a number of well-established societies, including the 'civilized Athenians' – the ethical principle and the utilitarian calculus come down to the same result.

In *The Wealth of Nations* there is no longer a need for such sophistication. The only criterion for an action's acceptability is its compatibility with the functioning of society. As already mentioned, the link with an ethical point of view now constructs itself in a more indirect manner.

There are numerous other passages in *The Theory of Moral Sentiments* that consider the opposition between ethics and morality. One of the best known is the first appearance of the invisible hand, whose general function will be discussed in Chapter 4. What matters here is the conflict between ethics and morality. The behaviour of the rich landowner, whose consumption of luxury goods in the 'gratification of his vain and insatiable desires' employs thousands of workmen, is unethical. It would never find approbation in the eyes of the impartial spectator. It is, however, morally acceptable since it ensures general well-being and thus provides the basis for the 'multiplication of the species' (Smith 1759 (IV.1.10): 215).

We pointed out above that the progressive retreat of an ethical point of view goes hand in hand with an ever closer control of the original passions. As is frequently the case with Adam Smith, form follows functions. Differences in the attitude towards the treatment of passions are reflected in the different styles of the two books. While the general tone of *The Theory of Moral Sentiments* is that of a philosophical discussion, Smith still permits himself the expression of personal sentiments. The style varies with a certain nervous energy between exhortation of the reader, logical argument and historical or literary exemplification. One comes away with the impression that only the irregular partitioning of the text into separate paragraphs of highly differing length, varying between several lines and several pages, accompanied by a complex structure of chapters and sub-chapters, can do justice to the multiple separate arguments that nevertheless all refer to each other at different moments.

In *The Wealth of Nations*, the tone has clearly changed. The narrator now assumes a much greater distance from the reader. The stylistic range has been reduced and the rhythm of the text, alternating between practical example and theoretical explication, is calm and clear. Smith no longer counts on rhetorical fireworks or emotional appeals to convince the reader, but relies on the evidence of a good explication of the social mechanism. Although the structure of the chapters is still not perfectly homogenous, it presents a far more regular frame for a calmly evolving argument. Finally, the analysis in *The Wealth of Nations* of a horizontal world, ruled by conventional values whose observation will achieve social well-being, is put forward in a detached and neutral tone that occasionally can become cold and pedantic. The book exemplifies Bergson's observations that 'pleasure and well-being are something indeed; [but that] joy is more' (Bergson 1932: 57).

However, despite the evident contrasts between the two books that allow characterising *The Theory of Moral Sentiments* as being shaped by the conflict between an ethical and a moral position and *The Wealth of Nations* as being constructed on the basis of an all-pervasive social morality, one should never underestimate the sophistication of Adam Smith's thought that permanently explores the boundary that separates ethical behaviour from moral behaviour. For instance, certain passages of *The Theory of Moral Sentiments* present to the reader ethical behaviour of the highest order, inspired by a desire to please the impartial spectator, and yet, they already contain a seed of ironic questioning that will later grow into the wholesale rejection of the possibility of such behaviour. In this context, Adam Smith frequently works with historical examples highlighting the valour of the ancient Greeks and Romans who follow their ethical ideals with stoic heroism. The following example is typical of the subtleness of the treatment that Smith imparts to them:

> Cato, surrounded on all sides by his enemies, unable to resist them, disdaining to submit to them, and reduced by the proud maxims of that age, to the necessity of destroying himself … arming himself with manly fortitude, and the moment before he executes his fatal resolution, giving with his usual tranquillity, all necessary orders for the safety of his friends, appears to Seneca, that great preacher of insensibility, a spectacle which even the gods themselves might behold with pleasure and admiration.
>
> (Smith 1759 (I.III.1.13): 58–59)

At a first level of reading, one cannot help but thinking that Smith proffers the example of a heroic act, beholden to no one but wishing to maintain identity with one's chosen values, which indeed the gods themselves would regard with pleasure and admiration. And yet, a closer look permits discerning an Adam Smith who, already at this point, is deeply sceptical of the great men of historical tradition and their ethical heroism. The value of ethical behaviour is thus already questioned at the level of the concrete case, when at a principle level the value of such behaviour is still recognised. In the passage cited, terms such as 'reduced by the maxims of that age', 'great preacher of insensibility' or even 'spectacle' create considerable distance for readers who would like to take Cato's ideals too literally. Another passage expresses

Smith's scepticism towards historic idealisation with breathtaking audacity:

> Had Cæsar, instead of gaining, lost the battle of Pharsalia, his character would, at this hour, have ranked a little above that of Catiline …
>
> (Smith 1759 (VI.III.29): 297)

And yet, the following paragraph recognises fully, without the slightest trace of irony, Cesar's true ethical virtues. Adam Smith never confuses 'praise' and 'praise-worthiness':

> His real merit, the justness of his taste, the simplicity and elegance of his writings, the propriety of his eloquence, his skill in war, his resources in distress, his cool and sedate judgment in danger, his faithful attachment to his friends, his unexampled generosity to his enemies, would all have been acknowledged.
>
> (Smith 1759 (VI.III.29, 297)

At each and every moment, Adam Smith escapes too simplistic an interpretation. Ethics and morality, the vertical principle and the horizontal principle, the impartial spectator and the sympathy mechanism, rejection of a 'moral sense' and preservation of its heritage, intertwine in his work. They are never completely separated and yet remain always fully distinct. If one looks for further corroboration of this constitutive tension in Smith's work, a look at his biography further highlights key aspects.

Mingling textual analysis and biographical considerations is always fraught with the risk of unduly projecting the structure of one – or what the critic might take for it – on the other. This usually provides distorted views of both, since a published book and a lived life spring from entirely different genetic rules. Elaboration of a text in the social sciences remains largely a conscious or, at most, semi-conscious activity, while understanding the essential lines of one's destiny is beyond the grasp of most. And yet, several aspects of Adam Smith's life are so peculiar from the point of view of the preceding discussion that wilfully omitting them would deprive the reader of what is perhaps not the final key to the understanding of Smith's work, but at the very least a set of interesting and instructive facts.

With these *caveats*, one can in fact see the life of Adam Smith as being similarly crossed by two different axes of orientation. Both are as indispensable, as they are incompatible at the level of daily practice.

Professor Adam Smith, the man who convinced the world more than anybody else before or after him of the benefits of free markets, laissez-faire and minimal government, completed his professional career from 1778 onwards as the head of the Royal fiscal administration of Scotland in Edinburgh. The contemporary title of this position was 'Comptroller of customs'. 'Comptroller of customs' had also been the profession of Adam Smith's father, albeit at a lower administrative level, in the nearby town of Kirkcaldy. Two other facts about Adam Smith's father are noteworthy. First, he bore the same name, Adam Smith, as his famous son. Second Adam Smith Jr. never got to know his forebear, since his father died before his son's birth (Rae 1895: 13). As is well known, Adam Smith Jr. subsequently lived most of his life – exceptions are his student years and the travels in France – next to his mother, who only died six years before his own death.

In the discussion of Smith's treatment of the figure without a definitive proper name that we refer to today as the impartial spectator, we had alluded to the notion of the 'name of the father' as the first and fundamental symbolic relationship that subsequently enables all others. While Lacanian psychoanalysis, which has introduced the term, is very clear about the fact that the 'father' of the 'name of the father' is not necessarily or not even primarily the real father, he does, nevertheless, have an important role to play in this context. In the words of Laurent Assoun:

> The real father supports as a "modest person" the symbolic function, to the extent that he manages to function as a symbolic father, who strictly speaking does not exist – that is: not in any form other than as function ... .
>
> (Assoun 2003: 52, our translation)

Providing a 'symbolic function', the possibility to sustain symbolic relationships means providing the possibility of developing an idea of the self that is of a different nature from the mirror image we receive from our friends, partners, competitors or peers. Lacan's work on the link between different structures of signification and different aspects of the human psyche (the domain of the symbolic, as well as the domain of the imaginary) relies in final instance on Roman Jakobson's work on the different axes of communication established by metaphor and metonymy as outlined in his celebrated article on 'Linguistics and Poetics' (Jakobson 1987).

Assoun's observation allows a further important insight in this context. The real father plays a key supporting role in the establishment of the symbolic function, but he is not identical with it. As we have already pointed out, Adam Smith, the philosopher and economist, is perfectly capable of handling symbolic figures of speech and does so with great dexterity, if not always with ultimate commitment. We do not know who precisely provided the necessary 'support' of which Assoun speaks. Rae mentions an uncle playing an important role in the child's upbringing; one might surmise that later teachers and friends contributed their share.

And yet, let us make no mistake: the defining feature of *The Wealth of Nations* is the radical and hitherto unheard of claim that societies work better when they forego the use of their symbolic function linked to history, power and a sense of identity shaped in the dialectical process between desire and language. Societies should modestly limit themselves to representing the outcome of the auto-organisation of their constituents by way of exchanging closed, iconic signifiers that have been found useful for establishing reciprocal 'sympathetic' reactions capable of providing an alternative form of identity. In short, Adam Smith presents the first complete blueprint of a purely horizontal, a fatherless, world.

It is obvious that Smith was not working in isolation and that in a particular radical fashion he developed one of the great faultlines of enlightenment thinking. Nevertheless, it is hard to avoid the conjecture that only his own peculiar personal experience would shape his genius in a manner that would have him, first, stage the battle over the privilege of setting behavioural norms between the impartial spectator and the sympathy mechanism and, second, allow him to think through a fatherless world with all its implications. Be this as it may, what is undeniable is that the opposition between a vertical and a horizontal axis and their complex articulation defines the heart of Smith's oeuvre. Subsequent generations of readers and commentators have at least implicitly recognised this by placing the image of the 'invisible hand' firmly at the centre of their discussions.

The recourse to biographical facts and their analogy to certain elements of the interpretation we propose evidently do not explain the particular genius of the son of the prematurely deceased fiscal administrator of Kirkcaldy. The structure of his unusual personal trajectory, however, permits us to rediscover the tensions defining his work. Only by way of a vast detour, that included the invention of a world in which all individual ethical projects had made way for an unconditional adherence to an inter-subjective morality, could Adam Smith construct his own *ethical project*.

Adam Smith not only creates a new scientific discipline and becomes, according to James Bonar's expression 'the Great Founder', but he will complete his career by adopting the profession of his father. In the only manner possible for him, by brandishing a society of peers, of brothers, of sons, and by exploring its foundations and its implications with patience, ardour and genius, Adam Smith Jr. advances towards his unknown father by becoming in his turn 'Comptroller of customs'. Handling the tension between these two opposing but inseparable poles with diligence and an unrivalled sense of balance has allowed Adam Smith's oeuvre to play its historic role and to maintain the interest of its readers for almost 250 years.

4 The paradoxical synthesis

4.1 'Efficient causes' and 'final causes': the working of the invisible hand

Chapters 2 and 3 of this book presented, respectively, the world of sympathy and the world of the impartial spectator. Each of these worlds has its own purpose and practice. Broadly speaking, *The Theory of Moral Sentiments* deals with the conflict between two normative orientations and *The Wealth of Nations* develops the vision of a world shaped by auto-organisation, for which the sympathy mechanism provides the essential basis in terms of motivation and process. And yet, neither *The Theory of Moral Sentiments* nor *The Wealth of Nations* can be reduced to a one-dimensional system constructed from a single set of first principles. Nor does either book offer the reader a choice between two distinct options. The reader is not even offered a middle road, a compromise. Adam Smith's final position is elaborated by means of a dialectical movement at different levels between these two frameworks.

Far too often, the secondary literature on *The Wealth of Nations* has been devoted to the identification of elements that question the dominance of economic criteria by highlighting a number of critical remarks of the author about the reality of market economies. Viner is an early and influential example of this tendency, but so are Diatkine, Young and many others. The implication of this procedure is that Smith was not a radical liberal but a sort of middle-of-the road social democrat. As supporting evidence are usually cited the passages concerning price fixing by people of the same trade meeting socially (Smith 1776 (I.10.2)) and the corrupting effects of the division of labour (Smith 1776 (V.1.3.2)).

Despite the intrinsic interest of these passages, it would be wrong to see them as a sign of a return to an ethical orientation that would relativise the dominance of economic behaviour shaped by social morality. These passages owe everything to Smith's realism and nothing to the re-establishment of a vertical principle. In fact, Smith cites the two instances as collateral damage of a market society that is certainly regrettable but does not question the dominance of the horizontal principle. Let us recall that demanding only 'second-best' behaviour, which is positive, realistic and attainable, is one of the defining features of the horizontal principle. The ethical element continues to exist, but it exists for Smith at another level – the level of the final outcome of the economic system. Paradoxically, the Smithian individual will satisfy his ethical impetus by adhering to the conventional values codified by the sympathy mechanism, since this is the mechanism created by the impartial spectator to achieve his objectives. This may be small comfort, but the quiet knowledge of having acted in conformity with the plan of the Director of nature is the only satisfaction he may hope to attain in this domain.

This structure of argument applies not only to abstract philosophical considerations but to concrete questions of social and economic behaviour. It is also behind the functioning of the 'invisible hand', which has become a notion of general culture, and quite rightly so, since it captures the essence of Adam Smith's legacy. The standard formula that the 'pursuit of self-interest promotes the general interest' reinforces, by way of its openly paradoxical nature, the fascination with the underlying proposition. While Adam Smith never expressed matters in such a set-piece manner, the formula of self-interest ensuring general interest captures his essential point quite well.

And yet, the image of the invisible hand remains mysterious. Even a diligent reading of Adam Smith's text does not allow resolving the simile with the help of an elegant analogy to dispel the mystery of the paradox. Any real paradox, however, possesses a solution, which is what distinguishes it from a contradictory double proposition. It is not for want of trying that no simple solution to the paradox has been found so far: from the hand of God to that of 'self-love', the original image has spawned a large number of secondary metaphors. Frequently, however, these images tell more about the respective critic and his preferences than about the functioning of the Smithian system. See, for instance, Prévost (2002b) or Dupuy (1988).

Other critics seek to elucidate the mystery by studying the possible origins of the image. Nobody has gone through Adam Smith's library in search of these origins with more diligence than Emma Rothschild. In *Economic Sentiments: Adam Smith, Condorcet and the*

Enlightenment (Rothschild 2003), she assembles a number of interesting leads. There exists, for instance, a passage from Shakespeare's *Macbeth* that makes reference to the invisible hand of night. When, after the murder of King Duncan, Macbeth commands that his accomplice Banquo also be killed he tells his wife who inquires about his projects in Scene 2 of Act 3:

> Be innocent of the knowledge, dearest chuck, Till thou applaud the deed. Come, seeling night; scarf up the tender eye of pitiful day; and with thy bloody and invisible hand, cancel and tear to pieces that great bond, which keeps me pale!
>
> (Shakespeare 1994: 85)

Another citation can be found in Voltaire's *Oedipe* in which the invisible hand of a superior force threatens the hero. From several passages in *The Theory of Moral Sentiments* it transpires that Smith appreciated Voltaire and knew his writings well. Finally, in Smith's edition of Ovid's *Metamorphoses* is a picture in which the invisible hand of a centaur wounds a warrior (all from Rothschild 2003: 118). Each one of these citations reveals a different facet of Adam Smith, who lectured as professor in Glasgow, of course, also on 'Rhetoric and Belles Lettres'. None of them, however, allows a definite understanding of the functioning of the invisible hand in Smith's work, primarily because this approach is based on the slightly facile assumption that Smith's literary culture immediately offers insight into the strategies of his texts. In the end, this procedure continues the fruitless search for a secondary metaphor for the image of the invisible hand, as if this could explain the autonomous working of this mysterious device that as *deus ex machina* operates the otherwise inexplicable transformation of self-interest into general interest. Only an approach that voluntarily abstains from looking for such *exogenous* explanations but limits itself to looking at the *internal* working of Smith's argumentation at the level of the texts themselves can hope to resolve the paradox at whose centre sits the invisible hand.

It is not by accident that the invisible hand and its contribution to aligning self-interest and general interest symbolises Adam Smith's essential contribution. The invisible hand sits indeed at the decisive juncture of his work. Firmly rooted in the horizontal world, one of its functions is to ensure that agents continue behaving according to their *horizontal* logic, while its strategic orientation remains the realisation of the objectives of the impartial spectator. Even if the invisible hand is only mentioned three times in all of the writings of

Adam Smith, its position at the very intersection of the horizontal and the vertical world confers to it an importance that is crucial – in the literal as well as the figurative sense of the word – for Smith's overall design.

The expression 'invisible hand' appears only once in *The Theory of Moral Sentiments* and once in *The Wealth of Nations.* It also appears once, and in chronological order the first time, as 'the invisible hand of Jupiter' in the manuscript of Smith's *History of Astronomy.* In this passage, uncultured observers ascribe otherwise inexplicable natural phenomena such as lightning to the invisible hand of the god. In our context, its appearance in *The Theory of Moral Sentiments* is the most significant one. Its mentioning in *The Wealth of Nations* is primarily a repetition which, however, contains an important additional precision. In *The Theory of Moral Sentiments,* it is the luxury consumption of a rich landowner that increases the welfare of the population due to the invisible hand. In *The Wealth of Nations* this idea is refined by having the invisible hand perform its task in the context of a multitude of profit-seeking individuals in competitive markets.

To understand the working of the invisible hand at the intersection of the two dimensions that structure Smith's world, one needs to step back to consider the distinction between 'efficient causes' and 'final causes' to which it is inevitably linked.[1] Efficient causes for Smith are emotional, physical or biological drivers which set in motion a man, a watch or the circulation of blood (all examples provided by Adam Smith). The link between an efficient cause and its effect is direct, inevitable and immediate. It is purely mechanical.

A final cause, instead, is a precise objective defined by a superior intelligence. The latter *uses* an efficient cause in order to better achieve its objective, the final cause. Such an objective may be simply 'telling the hour' for which a watchmaker would create a watch. In the context of the invisible hand, the final cause is general welfare, or the 'public interest' as Smith refers to it, and the propagation of the species. One could also say that the distinction between efficient cause and final cause, corresponds to the distinction between instrument and objective. A crucial point is that an efficient cause entirely ignores the final cause it serves. In fact, the less it knows about its purpose, the better it will accomplish it:

> The wheels of the watch are all admirably adjusted to the end for which it was made, the pointing of the hour. All their various motions conspire in the nicest manner to produce this effect.

> If they were endowed with a desire and intention to produce it, they could not do it better. Yet we never ascribe any such desire or intention to them, but to the watch-maker, and we know that they are put into motion by a spring, which intends the effect it produces as little as they do.
>
> (Smith 1759 (II.II.3.5): 102)

This is rather straightforward and quite banal when talking about the mechanics of watch-making. Nobody will challenge the fact that the wheels of a watch have no conscience of what they are doing. It is quite another matter, if the same reasoning is transposed in a perfectly analogue manner to human behaviour, its motivations and consequences. However, this is precisely the step that Adam Smith demands from his readers:

> But though, in accounting for the operations of bodies, we never fail to distinguish in this manner the efficient from the final cause, in accounting for those of the mind we are very apt to confound these two different things with one another. When by natural principles we are led to advance those ends, which a refined and enlightened reason would recommend to us, we are very apt to impute to that reason, as to their efficient cause, the sentiments and actions by which we advance those ends and to imagine that to be the wisdom of man, which in reality is the wisdom of God.
>
> (Smith 1759 (II.II.3.5): 102)

Only God knows the best means, the best efficient cause, to advance the final cause his wisdom has defined, that is general welfare. This means is the reliance on ‘natural principles’, a notion we shall come back to further below. The matter is, however, further complicated by the following subtlety: while Smith denies that humans have a choice in promoting the final cause, he clearly considers them capable of appreciating it. ‘Refined and enlightened reason’ can thus even *recommend* a final cause, but it has no role in ultimately selecting and promoting it. The direct and conscious pursuit of the objectives of the impartial spectator, even if fully understood and accepted, would constitute a dangerous adventure due to the hubris of equating human and divine wisdom.

It is the indirect route, by way of pursuing a socially formatted self-interest, that constitutes a far safer and more promising approach. In fact, the wisdom of God has, to this effect, designed a number of emotional stimuli that act as efficient causes and allow for attaining the final cause in a precise and mechanical way. Human reason, on the other hand, will be ignorant of this mechanism. Smith considers, very explicitly, that the personal instincts that function as efficient causes are unconscious. In a very modern sense, they are forces in the emotional economy of the individual that are unknown to the individual himself. And yet, men flatter themselves by claiming to have free will. One may think of this situation as if humans were strapped to the hands of the watch that Smith mentions, free to think what they like, but in reality dependent on the underlying movement they cannot but follow.

Typical of the roundabout nature of Adam Smith's way of proceeding, the decisive passage that explicitly details the mode of interaction between the Author of nature and humankind is hidden in a colossal footnote of over two pages in length. Human nature is presented here as an instrument crafted by God to better allow humans to accomplish his designs, which are in this passage 'self-preservation and the propagation of the species'. For Smith this human nature, which is considered part of nature proper, is here characterised by a utilitarianism structured by automatic behavioural stimuli. And yet, humans have not only 'desire' for immediate personal satisfaction but also for the overarching purpose of which they are part. This passage very much prepares the figure of the invisible hand. Given its importance for understanding the fundamental structure of Adam Smith's work, we will cite substantial parts of it:

> Though man, therefore, be naturally endowed with a desire of the welfare and the preservation of society, yet the Author of nature has not entrusted it to his reason to find out … the most proper means of attaining this end … The oeconomy of nature … has constantly in this manner not only endowed mankind with an appetite for the end which she proposes, but likewise with an appetite for the means by which alone this end can be brought about, for their own sakes, and independent of their tendency to produce it. Thus self-preservation, and the propagation of the species, are the great ends which Nature seems to have proposed in the formation of all animals … But though we are in this manner endowed with a very strong desire for those ends, it has not been intrusted to the slow and uncertain determinations of our reasons, to find out the proper means of bringing them about. Nature has directed us to the greater part of these by original and immediate instincts. Hunger, thirst, the passion which unites the two sexes,

> the love of pleasure, and the dread of pain, prompt us to apply those means for their own sakes, and without any consideration of their tendency to those beneficient ends which the great Director of nature intended to produce by them.
>
> (Smith 1759 (II.I.5.10): 90–91)

In the cited passage, Adam Smith distinguishes two potential forms of motivation for human actions aiming to achieve a given objective, a final cause. The first is a conscious motivation that chooses both the objective *and* the means for attaining it, in other words both the final and the effective cause. The second form of motivation is, at least partly, unconscious. While the final cause, the ultimate design of the Director of nature, might be intuited, humans have no means for hastening its realisation by choosing the appropriate efficient cause. Smith enumerates the needs or desires that will act as efficient causes outside of individual control and realise the final cause – hunger, thirst, the 'passion that unites the sexes', the love of pleasure, the dread of pain. Unsurprisingly, he associates these physical needs in a subsequent passage with 'natural hopes and fears, and suspicions … propagated by sympathy, and confirmed by education' (Smith 1759 (III.5.4): 191). These natural needs, hopes and fears constitute the 'viceregents' of the impartial spectator that impress their laws of movement on the Smithian individuals. They do so, not by influencing conscious choice, but indirectly, by way of physical or emotional necessity.

As mentioned above, we encounter the same idea according to which an unconscious stimulus originates an individual action attaining a socially 'beneficient' end in the famous passage introducing the division of labour at the beginning of *The Wealth of Nations* (Smith 1776 (I.2): 17). The division of labour 'from which so many advantages are derived, is not originally the effect of any human wisdom … [but] the necessary … consequence of … the propensity to truck, barter, and exchange one thing for another' (ibid.). As an extension of the sympathy mechanism, the underlying desire to exchange, sets in motion the system devised by the impartial spectator, who at this point has already withdrawn far into the background.

Human needs and emotions are thus opposed to human reason that attempts to identify itself consciously with the objectives of the impartial spectator. These needs and emotions will be more useful as 'efficient causes' than conscious reason. Both, physical desires such as hunger or sexual desire as well as emotions such as hope and fear, are associated with Smith's original notion of the passions.

They constitute the primary material for the sympathy mechanism, which moderates them into appropriate, socially acceptable sentiments. These sentiments allow the reassuring identification with one's peers. Physical desires and imagination are, in fact, relatively close in Smith's vision of the working of the human mind.

Both, the primary sentiments, or passions, and the secondary, sympathetic sentiments, are opposed by their unconscious nature to conscious reason identifying itself with the objectives of the impartial spectator. An essential qualification is warranted here: what is unconscious in the sympathetic sentiments is not their physical or moral object, which is consciously perceived, but the underlying desire for social conformity that has induced the Smithian individual to select the most widely accepted choice.

This combination of operative motivations that are structural and unconscious, on the one hand, and of conscious reason capable of making discrete choices over a limited set of options, on the other, is at the origin of economic rationality. The *homo oeconomicus* presented to the reader in *The Wealth of Nations* (without being addressed as such) results from the distrust of the Director of nature regarding the ability of his creation to stay faithful to his great design on the basis of personal reasoning. He thus makes men dependent on the proper means to achieve this design in addition to their unreliable love for the design itself. Once these means, the physical desires, yes, but more importantly the overarching desire for social recognition, have been put in place, a highly developed operational rationality will maximise wealth, the surest way to achieve this recognition. The price to pay is abandoning any idea of an operative constructive rationality. This peculiar vision of the working of the human mind, which combines the highest operational rationality in the pursuit of a well-defined programme with a complete inability to abandon or question this programme, is at the basis of establishing economics as a scientific discipline.

The above passage is thus rich in methodological and epistemological implications for the study of social behaviour in general and economics in particular. The distinction between efficient causes and final causes goes hand in hand with the distinction between a positive and a normative approach to social phenomena. Studying the efficient causes, which are associated with the 'original and immediate instincts' mentioned above, is equivalent to an objective, positive approach, precisely because their working remains outside of the control of the individuals under study. Studying the final causes and the objectives of the impartial spectator implies value judgements and a normative approach. Smith was fully aware of this and introduced the above passage with the following words:

> Let it be considered too, that the present inquiry is not concerning a matter of right, if I may say so, but concerning a matter of fact. We are not at present examining upon what principles a perfect being would approve of the punishment of bad actions [the topic of the preceding paragraph]; but upon what principles so weak and imperfect a creature as man actually and in fact approves of it.
>
> (Smith 1759 (II.I.5.10): 90)

The *homo œconomicus*, mechanically maximising his utility independent of any conscious decision of his own, is born with Adam Smith. Once Smith has decided focussing on the efficient causes, he initiates 'positive economics' (see, for example, Friedman 1953). Of course, *homo œconomicus* 'chooses' the quantity and quality of the goods he sells, buys or consumes, but de does so only to the extent that he follows the preordained programme the Director of nature has designed for him. The scientific character of economics hinges on the solidity of this assumption. This assumption has found its modern, secular expression in the 'methodological individualism' of the Chicago school, which assigns to the genetic code the role that Smith reserved for the impartial spectator.

4.2 The invisible hand and the 'cunning of reason'

Once the interaction between 'efficient causes' and 'final causes' is understood, one can determine with precision the working of the invisible hand. In fact, the invisible hand does nothing else than to ensure that the efficient cause of socially formatted self-interest realises the final cause of general well-being. The more completely men abandon themselves to the efficient cause, the faster the final cause will be attained in the roundabout way devised by the impartial spectator. Any attempt to attain the final cause directly would instead only weaken the efficient cause. Such an attempt would thus be counterproductive and should be proscribed. In fact, the final objective would be attained in the surest manner if any conscious notion of the final objective were to be abandoned, forgotten or veiled. Abandoning the ambition of personally identifying the ultimate finality of human interaction implies also abandoning all attempts at identifying with the impartial spectator. Instead of misguided human hubris, the silent working of the efficient cause of the profit motive will realise the final cause of general welfare.

And how does the invisible hand contribute to the realisation of this design? Chapter 2 in fact showed that the two fundamental hypotheses that Adam Smith employs – the codification of preferences through the sympathy mechanism and the establishment of competitive markets through the division of labour and the abolition of monopolies – are quite sufficient on their own to ensure general welfare. Two centuries of research on general economic equilibrium and the first fundamental theorem of welfare economics have confirmed Adam Smith's original intuition. What is there left to do? What function could the invisible hand possibly still assume?

A first function the invisible hand assumes is simply to respond to an expectation of additional signification, without in fact contributing anything new. The result postulated by Smith that the pursuit of self-interest is the best means to ensure general interest is so surprising – in particular, when the particularities of this self-interest are presented implicitly rather than explicitly – that this mystery seems to require a decisive, supplementary causal factor. Due to a limited understanding of the functioning of a market economy, there thus exists a gap in meaning that is addressed by the notion of the invisible hand. The invisible hand thus serves as a cipher, a symbol for a mechanism of auto-organisation, which is already perfectly defined and described but whose consequences are so momentous and surprising that they call forth an additional explanation. In this sense, the invisible hand is invisible because it does not exist. Its function is to capture a self-sufficient mechanism of auto-regulation in a captivating, synthetic picture in order to better convey its importance. This benign sleight-of-hand that consists of suggesting a distinct functional entity, where there exist in fact only the smoothly running mechanics of the social movements, corresponds to a need for simple but striking explanations of complex but prosaic phenomena. Adam Smith has perfectly described such a mechanism in his *History of Astronomy*, where he ascribes to 'savages' the need for invoking the 'invisible hand of Jupiter' in order to explain unusual or 'irregular' events that confound expectations:

> For it may be observed, that in all Polytheistic religions, among savages, as well as in the early ages of Heathen antiquity, it is the irregular events of nature only that are ascribed to the agency and power of their gods. Fire burns, and water refreshes; heavy bodies descend, and lighter substances fly upwards, by the necessity of their own nature; nor was the invisible hand of Jupiter ever apprehended to be employed in those matters. But thunder and

> lightning, storms and sunshine, those more irregular events, were ascribed to his favour, or his anger … And thus, in the first ages of the world, the lowest and most pusillanimous superstition supplied the place of philosophy.
>
> (Smith 1980: 49–50)

However, in satisfying a social demand with an inspired rhetorical figure, the image of the invisible hand fulfils a second function. This second function does not yet exist in *The History of Astronomy* but plays an important role in both *The Theory of Moral Sentiments* and *The Wealth of Nations.* Invisible because it is non-existent, the invisible hand suggests an autonomous operative entity where there is none (at least not at the level of any direct intervention into the market process). In doing so, it occupies the space and impedes any ill-advised alternative attempts at claiming the crucial intersection between the vertical and the horizontal axis. Such tranquillity is necessary to let the design of the Director of nature accomplish itself unperturbed and unobserved. This is precisely what the invisible hand ensures, veiling not only the final cause of the impartial spectator but more importantly the unconscious efficient causes that promote it, such as the desire for sympathy and social recognition, as well as the quest for wealth that comes with it. The invisible hand thus allows men to better abandon themselves to the pursuit of their socially beneficial self-interest codified by the sympathy mechanism.

Smith is perfectly clear about the fact that the process of promoting the general interest through the pursuit of self-interest can only succeed if it progresses unconsciously, 'without intention' and 'without knowing'. The sympathy mechanism can deploy its force only when men are ignorant about the ultimate objective of their actions. The benefits of ignorance and the abandonment of any constructive rationality are thus corollaries of the sympathy mechanism and assume an increasing importance during the course of *The Theory of Moral Sentiments* to the extent that the direct communication with the impartial spectator recedes. The near-total absence of any motivation of human behaviour other than the pursuit of self-interest becomes subsequently the hallmark of *The Wealth of Nations.*

Both books state identically that the invisible hand works only when 'intention' and 'knowledge' of the final outcome are absent in the pursuit of self-interest. The context carefully prepares these statements. The paragraphs that precede the famous passage with the first apparition of the invisible hand in *The Theory of Moral Sentiments* thus deal with the divergence between a good's objective utility, its use value, and its utility in the imagination of the owner, which will ultimately become part of the process of the formation of exchange value. As noted already in Chapter 1, according to Adam Smith the economic value of a good does not arise from its use value, that is the satisfaction of real needs, either physical needs and the need for 'peace of mind'. A good's value results from the esteem and the envy that it procures its owner. The 'parade of riches' flatters his vanity and satisfies his need to be loved, independently of the use value of his belongings.

The invisible hand works in this economy of appearance, representation and mutual recognition. The attention paid to the regard of their peers forces the rich to spend their funds in representative consumption goods and thus to contribute to general welfare. Smith quotes the proverb that 'the eye is larger than the belly' to underline that the driving force behind conspicuous consumption is seated in the imagination, not in the satisfaction of physical needs or pleasures. Given that direct consumption will quickly hit diminishing returns, a rich man will need to circulate his wealth to derive pleasure from it. The vanity of the rich and their desire for social recognition, the efficient causes, thus become the principal source of income for the broad mass of the poor, the final cause. Virtual satisfactions and imagination thus set in motion real and productive economic processes. The invisible hand just ensures that this peculiar economic set-up keeps on ticking over smoothly:

> The rich … consume little more than the poor, and in spite of their natural selfishness and rapacity, though they mean only their own conveniency … they divide with the poor the produce of all their improvements. They are led by an invisible hand to make nearly the same distribution of the necessaries of life, which would have been made, had the earth been divided into equal portions among all its inhabitants, and thus without intending it, without knowing it, advance the interest of the society, and afford means to the multiplication of the species … In ease of body and peace of mind, all the different ranks of life are nearly upon a level, and the beggar, who suns himself by the side of the highway, possesses that security which kings are fighting for.
>
> (Smith 1759 (IV.1.10): 215–16)

The true needs of rich and poor, of kings and beggars, are thus largely satisfied to the same extent. The use value at their disposal, consisting as always with Smith of physical comfort and a feeling of safety, is largely comparable. The difference between them resides in the standing they have in the eyes of their brethren, who venerate the rich and despise the poor. As we have seen in the chapters on the sympathy mechanism, this difference in social standing alone is the incentive behind the pursuit of 'self-interest' in terms of wealth maximisation. After all, wealth permits the satisfaction, at least temporarily, of that most essential of needs – to feel loved. Given also that the desirability of individual goods stems from their social effects, value is – beyond satisfying the most basic needs – exchange value.

A good is worth to me what it is worth in the eyes of my peers, who base their judgement on the aesthetic experience of a good's *perceived* usefulness. 'Of the beauty which the appearance of Utility bestows upon the characters and actions of men; and how far the perception of this beauty may be regarded as one of the original principles of approbation' is the programmatic title of the chapter following the introduction of the invisible hand in *The Theory of Moral Sentiments.* The fact that aesthetic perception or imagination dominates the actual experience of utility ensures the working of the social function of wealth. And it is by way of this social function of wealth, the conspicuous consumption and circulation of funds that come with it, that the invisible hand functions.

Whether one chooses to consider the overarching desire for social recognition as the ultimate efficient cause or the invisible hand of the Director of nature that has put it in place, comes down to personal preference. The invisible hand has occasionally been considered the 'hand of God', in reference to the passage in *History of Astronomy* (see Prévost (2002b)). More precisely, one might consider it as the hand of the Director of nature, also known as the impartial spectator. After all, the impartial spectator has put in place the mechanism that the invisible hand ensures. However, one needs to heed an important *caveat*, which immediately diminishes the intrinsic value of such an interpretation. The invisible hand does not *add* anything to the fundamental structures of human behaviour decided upon by the impartial spectator long ago. The invisible hand is not about any direct intervention of the impartial spectator in the economic process, but about shaping the process by giving humans 'eyes larger than their belly' which makes them appreciate exchange value over use value.

The passage cited above also confirms that the invisible hand 'leads' its subjects without revealing to them the ultimate finality of their actions. 'Without intending' and 'without knowing' these actions advance the socially beneficial ends of the economic process. This should not come as a surprise; the less an efficient cause is aware of the final cause it is designed to serve, the better it is able to function. It is better to hide the futility of the rich landowner's quest for social standing from himself, as the underlying structure of his personal utility function operates best in an unconscious manner. The invisible hand thus maintains a useful veil of ignorance.

The theme of 'not intending' and 'not knowing' is reiterated in the passage that introduces the invisible hand in *The Wealth of Nations*. Here, Adam Smith elaborates explicitly on this theme by explicitly castigating conscious attempts to advance the 'public good':

> As every individual, therefore, endeavours as much as he can both to employ his capital in the support of domestic industry, and so to direct that industry that its produce may be of the greatest value; every individual necessarily labours to render the annual revenue of the society as great as he can. Indeed, he generally neither intends to promote the public interest, nor knows how much he is promoting it. By preferring the support of domestic to that of foreign industry, he intends only his own security; and by directing that industry in such a manner as its produce may be of the greatest value, he intends only his own gain, and he is in this, as in many other cases, led by an invisible hand to promote an end which was no part of their intention. Nor is it always the worse for the society that it was no part of it. By pursuing his own interest he frequently promotes that of society more effectually than when he really intends to promote it. I have never heard much good done by those who affected to trade for the public good.
>
> (Smith 1776 (IV.II): 477–78)

The formulaic phrase attributed to Milton Friedman that 'the social responsibility of business is to increase its profits' perfectly resumes without a trace of irony Adam Smith's thinking on this point. Personal negotiations with the impartial spectator or creative generosity threatening to deconstruct society's silent movements would only disturb the codification of preferences and the frictionless circulation of wealth.[2]

Once more the indirect route towards the final cause is the safer, and ultimately, the only acceptable one. The direct route is based on 'moral sense' and an interior dialogue with the impartial spectator. It presupposes a conscience of one's actions, their motivation and their consequences. It is considered a noble but elitist choice in *The Theory of Moral Sentiments* and a dangerous presumption in *The Wealth of Nations.* The second route is based on the sympathy mechanism and the invisible hand. This route is based on the divergence between a subjective perception of the facts ('wealth procures happiness') and reality ('wealth procures few true satisfactions but flatters our vanity by inciting the envy of others and providing increased social standing'). Once consciousness is thus reduced to a purely operational rationality to maximise wealth, the pursuit of self-interest on the basis of well-codified preferences ensures general welfare.

The Smithian system is based on an ignorance of the origin and destiny of one's actions that is guaranteed by the invisible hand. One advances the general interest only to the extent that one does not intend to do so. The invisible hand adds nothing to individuals' actions but eliminates the knowledge of what they are doing. This ignorance of the final objective is necessary for the promotion of general welfare. The knowledge of this final objective of an economic system based on the pursuit of individual self-interest, the maximisation of social welfare, is from now on reserved for those who know *that one must not use this knowledge* – that is to say economists and, in particular, liberal economists.

Adam Smith's liberalism is motivated by the complex system of causalities the Director of nature has established to achieve his objective of general well-being. For Adam Smith, this objective motivates the means to realise it – economic liberalism. In *The Wealth of Nations*, the systematic and enthusiastic exploration of this originally ancillary process gains a certain degree of autonomy. Nevertheless, one should not consider Adam Smith's liberalism as a preference formulated a priori. Liberalism and the pursuit of economic self-interest remain his answers to the question of what is the best manner for enabling social life to produce lasting benefits for the community as a whole. Once the answer has been defined, any interference with the autonomous movements of the individual agents directed by the efficient causes would only endanger the final cause. Consequently, Adam Smith refuses any creative, constructivist rationality or political project threatening to interfere with the stable codification of preferences and the predictable flows of the unconscious motivation to achieve the recognition of one's peers:

> The man of system … is apt to be very wise in his own conceit … He does not consider that … in the great chessboard of human society, every single piece has a principle of motion of its own, altogether different from that which the legislature might chuse to impress upon it.
>
> (Smith 1759 (VI.II.2.17): 275)

The structure of Adam Smith's paradoxical argumentation concerning the functioning of the invisible hand was later generalised by Georg Wilhelm Friedrich Hegel in his *History of Philosophy* with the notion of the 'cunning of reason'. In Hegel as in Smith, the 'particular interests of passion' unconsciously achieve the designs of a 'general idea' according to a preset plan. Both have been defined by 'reason' (*Vernunft)* which *mutatis mutandis* is an abstract reincarnation of the impartial spectator without his ability to constitute the internalised subject of conscience. Reason in the Hegelian conception abstains, from the start, from any direct intervention in the movement of the passions transformed into particular interests. And despite the fact that in Hegel's approach these particular interests partly perish in the dialectical process of their realisation, while in Smith's approach emulation preserves them intact, the result is the same:

> The particular interest of passion is thus inseparable from the affirmation of the general [interest]; because the general results from the particular and the definite and from its negation. The particular exhausts itself in reciprocal struggle and part of it will perish. It is not the general idea, which enters into contradiction and struggle, imperilling itself; untouched and unharmed it remains in the background. This is to be called the *cunning of reason*, that it lets the *passions* act on its behalf, a process in which the elements through which it manifests itself will be diminished and damaged.
>
> (Hegel 1986: 49, our translation)[3]

5 Conclusion

The ethics of morality

The present reading of Adam Smith's work revealed an abundance of different leads, hints, tentative explorations, qualifications and concessions. It is time now to insist once more on its profound coherence. This coherence both transcends, and depends on, the fundamental dichotomy that runs through Smith's work.

This dichotomy once more concerns, of course, the relation between the vertical dimension and the horizontal dimension. The first is defined by the exogenous norms of the impartial spectator allowing the development of a personal ethic. The second is defined by the endogenous moral norms created by the sympathy mechanism. It was shown that the dominance of the horizontal dimension and the sympathy mechanism allowed for the codification of economic values. In its purest form, such codification attains an iconic signification in which sign and meaning confound themselves. The elimination of informational transaction costs that comes with this codification establishes the world of competitive markets of *The Wealth of Nations.*

At a second level, however, this predominance of the horizontal dimension will allow the realisation of the original promise connected with an observation of the commandments of the impartial spectator. The withdrawal of the impartial spectator thus permits the realisation of his project to guarantee general welfare and the propagation of the species. The totality of Adam Smith's published work must thus be understood as being profoundly unified by the sustained and realised effort of managing the tensions between the two normative systems that structure it.[1] Despite their mutual contribution to the unicity of Smith's oeuvre, the horizontal and vertical dimensions remain always perfectly distinct. Smith never aims for a compromise that would blur their distinctive features. This holds at the level of the direct determination of human behaviour as well as at the level of the finality of the intentions of the impartial spectator, or, in Smith's terms, at the level of the efficient as well as of the final causes.

One additional step remains to be taken, a final deepening, for the full comprehension of Adam Smith's work. The irreducible ambivalence, the dialectic, between the two dimensions is not only identifiable in the macrostructure of this work but also in its microstructure, occasionally in its very language. This double structure of the text at all levels strengthens both the coherence and the enduring attraction of Smith's work but also increases the difficulty of any linear interpretation. In both *The Theory of Moral Sentiments* and *The Wealth of Nations*, there exist bridges or points of direct contact between the horizontal axis of the world of sympathy and the vertical axis of the impartial spectator. These points of contact never question the fundamental irreducibility of the two axes but reflect on a smaller scale their intrinsically complementary nature, which establishes the internal coherence of the two books. Consider the following passage:

> The man within the breast, the abstract and ideal spectator of our sentiments and conduct, requires often to be awakened and put in mind of his duty, by the presence of the real spectator: and it is always from that spectator, from whom we can expect the least sympathy and indulgence, that we are likely to learn the most complete lesson of self-command.
>
> (Smith 1759 (III.III.38): 178)

The 'abstract and ideal spectator' can thus be 'awakened' by a real spectator who has more in common with the 'other', the peers or neighbours of the Smithian agent, with whom he enters into relations of sympathy, rather than with the abstract figure of the impartial spectator.

It is understandable that such a passage can confound certain critics when read out of context. It seems to support the idea that the impartial spectator is just one horizontal reference among others, just another 'bystander' in the terms of Jean-Pierre Dupuy. And yet, an accurate reading shows that this passage does not reduce the distinction between the two normative principles but rather reinforces it. In fact, the 'real spectator' in question in the above passage is not interested in a sympathetic relation. Smith instead points out that he aims at rousing the 'ideal spectator' inside ourselves to strengthen our 'self-command' and that we can precisely *not* expect any sympathy from him. The 'real spectator' above has thus two qualities. His physical likeness with the Smithian individual associates him with the horizontal sphere of similarity and sympathy. His regard without sympathy or indulgence exhorting to duty and self-command associates him with the vertical sphere of the impartial spectator. The fact that such distinct traits can be found in the same physical person, should not lead to confusing two fundamentally different functions.

Dupuy's follow-up suggestion that the impartial spectator just represents one point of view among many others blurs another essential difference between the two axes. The non-committal, random nature of certain choices, especially if considered from a point of view *ex ante*, belongs entirely to the horizontal sphere, while the vertical sphere is precisely characterised by its non-negotiable character committing an individual to one single choice if he wants to confirm his identity. Listening to the impartial spectator does not constitute just one possible additional choice, but implies an entirely different nature of decision-making than that of choosing between a multitude of equivalent choices established by the sympathetic process of reciprocal preference formation. Bergson and Ricœur have shown the irreducible difference between ethics and morals, teleology and deontology, joy and well-being that comes with these two distinct modes of making choices.

In the preceding chapters we have expressed this difference in the opposition between a symbolic and an iconic from of signification. The discrete choices emanating from the sympathy mechanism are always highly codified. The discovery of a personal choice in an open process, intimately linked to the history of the subject, his acquisition of language and values, is of an entirely different nature.

And yet, with Adam Smith, one can never oppose the two principles in too schematic a manner. The possibility of an 'orthogonalisation', the projection of a motive from one axis onto the other remains always possible, again without ever blurring their distinctive features:

> The virtues of prudence, justice, and beneficence, have no tendency to produce any but the most agreeable effects. Regard to those effects, as it originally recommends them to the actor, so does it afterwards to the impartial spectator … In our approbation of all those virtues, our sense of their agreeable effects, of their utility, either to the person who exercises them, or to some other persons, joins with our sense of their propriety … .
>
> (Smith 1759 (VI.Conclusion.6): 311)

The two principles can thus have identical 'local' implications while maintaining their distinctive features. One may ask, but if the two axes interact to accomplish general welfare *and* if they also can have, at least in certain circumstances, the same implications for individual behaviour, what is then their true difference? The answer is, of course, that they belong to fundamentally different processes of value generation with, notably, an entirely different informational structure of the values they generate.

The interweaving of the two dimensions is not limited to *The Theory of Moral Sentiments* but is continued in *The Wealth of Nations.* True, as was said earlier, direct manifestations of the impartial spectator cease to exist with the refutation of the notion of 'moral sense' and only his objective of general welfare survives as the final perspective for the interaction of the individual self-interests. The value system structured by the impartial spectator no longer directly determines human behaviour in *The Wealth of Nations.* These conclusions continue to be correct. *The Wealth of Nations* remains the panorama of a world structured by self-interest defined in terms of personal wealth maximisation.

And yet, the disappearance of direct manifestations of the impartial spectator in *The Wealth of Nations* is less complete than one might think. We already discussed in Chapter 3 the particular case of the virtue of justice associated with the impartial spectator and its continuing existence in a mundane, secular manifestation in the form of codified human law. The non-negotiable character of justice is maintained without any qualifications in *The Wealth of Nations,* where the pursuit of self-interest remains subordinated to the scrupulous observation of all legal requirements at all times.[2]

There exist additional traces of the impartial spectator in *The Wealth of Nations* beyond the legacy of obedience to the law. Jacob Viner in his famous article on 'Adam Smith and *Laissez faire*' (Viner 1928), for instance, strives hard to identify in Smith's work a spirit of compromise between the results of the auto-organisation of self-interested individuals and the general interest which is associated with well-intended government interventions. While Viner's article is rightly one of the classic contributions to the discussion of Adam Smith's work, he goes too far when identifying, on the basis of a number of exceptions to a pure market-based approach, a general compromise between the market and the *direct* realisation of the general interest. The essential contribution of *The Wealth of Nations* remains the demonstration that the roundabout process of pursuing economic self-interest is indeed the safest route to public welfare. Nevertheless, Viner identifies a residual ambivalence in the text that is worth exploring.[3]

The exceptions to a pure market orientation in *The Wealth of Nations* can be classed in two categories. The first category, on which Viner concentrates, contains all the government functions that Adam Smith considers admissible or even necessary for the functioning of a market economy. There is, of course, the administration of justice with the particular obligation to ensure physical safety, property rights and the honouring of contracts. Necessary government functions also include ensuring the stability of currency and, as a high priority, defence against foreign aggression ('defence … is of much more importance than opulence' (Smith 1776 (IV.II): 487). Despite their intrinsic importance, however, these government functions are only legitimised by establishing the necessary framework conditions for maintaining and facilitating a market economy. Even a 'horizontal' world requires 'vertical' elements, in particular with respect to the sanctity of contracts and the control of that residue of the passions that always threatens to erupt in physical violence. These functions therefore do not represent an essential divergence from the basic paradigm of *The Wealth of Nations*, which remains auto-organisation of wealth-maximising individuals with socially codified preferences.

There exists, however, a second, more surprising, category consisting of a small number of cases where Adam Smith goes beyond this ancillary function of 'vertical' elements and re-establishes a logic of action that responds to the demands of the impartial spectator – in explicit opposition to any arguments based on individual or even collective utility in terms of economic welfare. The first case, once a professor, always a professor, concerns the public financing of education at the primary school level. Applying the full force of his considerable rhetorical means, Smith demands that government ensure primary education *independently* of any utilitarian calculus:

> A man without the proper use of the intellectual faculties of a man, is, if possible, more contemptible than even a coward, and seems to be mutilated and deformed in a still more essential part of the character of human nature. Though the state was to derive no advantage from the instruction of the inferior ranks of people, it would still deserve its attention that they should not be altogether uninstructed.
>
> (Smith 1776 (V.I.3.2): 308–9)

The fact that Smith enumerates in the following a number of material advantages of primary education does not change the fact that his basic argument is based on an ethical imperative.

Smith's well-known remarks about the deforming effects of the division if labour are formulated in the same context. At decisive instances, the idea that man is more than the sum of the attributes he can bring to bear in the exchange of sentiments, values and commodities, thus also survives in *The Wealth of Nations.* But how is this idea compatible with a system whose ability to organise the mutual exchanges in a manner that maximises their general benefit, depends on the absence of any such 'overplus' as Smith would have called it? The two paradigms are compatible since Adam Smith distinguishes two phases – a phase of formation and definition and a phase of application and participation. The first phase serves to acquaint the individual with the array of possible goods and values and to form individual preferences differentiated by quantity even if not by quality. Once formed, the preferences remain stable. This phase is distinguished from the second phase, during which these preferences are applied in the network of social exchanges.

A social investment in primary education, contributing to develop men worthy of that designation, does not intervene in the second phase. It leaves individuals perfectly free to act according to their preferences without the slightest trace of any social engineering. On the contrary, one might argue that government-sponsored primary education, beyond its intrinsic merits, contributes to the basic skill set necessary for participating in a market economy.

Perhaps the most striking instance in *The Wealth of Nations,* in which Smith insists explicitly on the priority of an ethical stance over a point of view informed by social morality, concerns the question of slavery. In a unique passage, Adam Smith reintroduces a pre-eminent instance of justice, not unlike the 'great judge and arbiter', in the form of Emperor Augustus who limits the exercise of self-interest in the name of basic humanity. Smith introduces the passage carefully by developing, at some length, the opposition between 'arbitrary government' characterised by hierarchical relations and wanton bureaucratic interference (but capable of non-economic sentiments) and 'free government', essentially the market society he advocates throughout *The Wealth of Nations*:

> That the condition of a slave is better under an arbitrary than under a free government, is, I believe, supported by the history of all ages and nations … When Vedius Pollio, in the presence of Augustus, ordered one of his slaves, who had committed a slight fault, to be cut into pieces and thrown into his fish-pond to feed his fishes, the emperor commanded him, with indignation, to emancipate not only that slave, but all others that belonged to him. Under the republic no magistrate could have had authority enough to protect the slave, much less to punish the master.
>
> (Smith 1776 (IV.VII.2): 100–101)[4]

Typically, the incident happens in Roman times. Antiquity, for Smith, and not only for him, is the time for heroic behaviour informed by ethical prerogatives.

In the context of our discussion of the relationship between a moral and an ethical dimension, it is however worth highlighting that Smith is perfectly aware of the conflict his position provokes with the most fundamental principles of *The Wealth of Nations*:

> In every country where the unfortunate law of slavery is established, the magistrate, when he protects the slave, intermeddles in some measure in the management of the private property of the master; and, in a free country … he dare not do this but with the greatest caution and circumspection … But in a country where the government is in a great measure arbitrary, where it is usual for the magistrate to intermeddle even in the management of the private property of individuals, and to send them, perhaps, a letter de cachet if they do not manage it to his liking, it is much easier for him to protect the slave; and common humanity naturally disposes him to do so.
>
> (Smith 1759 (IV.VII.2): 100)

At first sight, the opposition between freedom and private property on the one hand and of arbitrary government and humanity on the other comes as a surprise. Do freedom and humanity not relate to each other? This opposition can only be understood in the perspective of the tension that runs through Adam Smith's work between a social morality articulated in free, but codified, markets and an ethic that is both universal and individual and thus discretionary. The freedom of disposing of one's private property and the liberty of the slave are thus associated with different, even conflicting value systems. Once more, the opposition between morality and ethics is driven by the question of whether the interest of society or the interest of the individual should have priority. There is no doubt that, from a social point of view, Adam Smith considers a 'free country' the best form of organisation. From the point of view of the suffering individual, arbitrary intervention, in the sense of the acting as an independent arbiter, leaves room for considerations other than utility maximisation in terms of socially formatted values.

The passages on primary education and slavery are the only ones in *The Wealth of Nations* where Adam Smith explicitly opposes an ethical imperative based on exogenous and autonomous values to the utilitarian arguments based on the endogenous morality of the sympathy mechanism. In the rest of the book, Adam Smith maintains, without exception, the dominance of conventional values resulting from social auto-organisation, which act as efficient causes that will attain the final objectives of the impartial spectator. Only in the two cited instances, the impartial spectator makes his presence felt directly again, briefly and in veiled but easily recognisable form. For the rest of the time since Hutcheson's 'moral sense' was refuted, the great Director of nature is happy to remain in the background and to let the 'particular interests of passion' work for him and the general interest.

Other passages mention, of course, historical or institutional barriers to the full realisation of a utilitarian logic based on auto-organisation. Jacob Viner enumerates a number of instances suggesting that Smith had a critical eye on market society in a large number of cases: conflicts between masters and workers, the habitual collusion of producers to fix prices or the fraudulent overestimation of future profits. However, these are shortcomings of market society only to the extent that they impede its full realisation. Frequently, these instances are cited disapprovingly; in other moments they are considered as inevitable shortcomings of human nature that one has to reckon with. They never question, however, the strategic perspective of the text, namely that future progress towards a more perfect market society is desirable.

To the extent possible, these imperfections need to be eliminated in order to accelerate progress towards the smooth movement of competitive markets, which alone is capable of ensuring general well-being. The inescapable side-effects of a market society never suggest the subordination of economic logic under an ethical imperative. In no other instance are they elevated to the rank of not only an acceptable but desirable exception from pure market logic as was the case for primary education and the humane treatment of slaves. In *The Wealth of Nations*, the two cited passages remain the only ones which imply the possibility that ethical considerations can and should supersede the values and behavioural structures formatted by the sympathy mechanism. Their very rareness makes them special.

And yet, the impartial spectator has left a further mark in *The Wealth of Nations* in a more subtle manner. That mark can be found in the style and the narrative structure of the book rather than in the topics it deals with. The attentive reader will have noted the change in tone when progressing from *The Theory of Moral Sentiments* to *The Wealth of Nations*. It is now more measured, more assured, less fiery than before. There is less place for doubt, but the price to pay is the absence of emotion, of passion, except, in fact, in the two passages cited above. The tone is voluntarily neutral, occasionally in an almost provocative manner when abstraction is made from individual calamities even in the most extreme circumstances. During long passages of *The Wealth of Nations*, it seems as if the impartial spectator made himself felt by his absence. The text reads on occasion like an illustration of Smith's assertion that 'the very suspicion of a fatherless world, must be the most melancholy of all reflections'. (Smith 1759 (VI.II.3.2): 277)

Finally, *The Wealth of Nations* contains homage to the impartial spectator, the Director of nature in the very figure of the narrator. It is the narrator who has the right to identify the intentions of the impartial spectator, that is to realise the general interest through the auto-organisation of individuals who are independent in terms of their immediate actions but share the same qualitative preferences and the same desire to acquire wealth in order to accede to generalised sympathetic recognition. This paradoxical figure of argument, where a conscious, external interpreter appreciates the results of a process accomplished by unconscious agents, is characteristic of all models of auto-organisation from Mandeville and Smith to Walras and Hayek. Whatever the extent of the *absence* of constructivist rationality, required for auto-organisation to succeed on the basis of unconscious, structural determinants, it requires a constructivist rationalist to appreciate the result. This privilege of interpretation and knowledge is even more precious, given that its utilisation or even injudicious communication could have nefarious consequences for the process of auto-organisation itself. In Adam Smith's world it remains far better for the average man to remain ignorant of the impartial spectator's final design in order to complete it.

This, however, does not hold for the author and narrator of *The Wealth of Nations*, who speaks with assurance to the rulers of this world. With calm authority, he explains that creating room for the exercise of economic self-interest and renouncing any misplaced ambition in terms of social engineering are the surest means to general welfare. He thus becomes the first exegete of the great book of nature that its Director has written and initiates a new scientific discipline.

After Adam Smith, his disciples and all those who, following in their footsteps, call themselves economists, claim the right to know the outcome of the unconscious movement of the self-interested agents. However, the more faithfully they follow their vocation, the less they have the right to use their knowledge. With *The Wealth of Nations,* an economist can hoist himself up to sit at Adam Smith's side on the elevated perch of those who know but do not intervene. *Laissez faire, laissez passer*, only the smooth movement of the blind pursuit of individual desire guarantees the common good. The initiated know this; however, they will forever be unable to employ their knowledge without betraying it.

Adam Smith handled the tension between clearly comprehending a final purpose and abstaining from all action to hasten it along, with an unusually acute sense of balance. He explored diligently all the subtleties of the argument without ever losing sight of the strategic objective of his paradoxical project: to describe a world, in which the impartial spectator, he whose name no one knows, effaces himself in order to ensure the success of his designs.

Notes

1 Introduction: personal ethics and social morality

1 For a first appreciation of the influence of Smith's work the two classic articles by Jacob H. Hollander, 'The Dawn of a New Science' and 'The Founder of a School', both in *Adam Smith, 1776 – 1926* (1928, 1989), are an excellent starting point. For a more complete appreciation, we suggest the volume by Andrew S. Skinner and Thomas Wilson (1975), *Essays on Adam Smith*, Oxford, Clarendon.

2 Quotations are referenced both according to the organisation of the text and the page. For *The Theory of Moral Sentiments*, Roman numerals thus indicate the book and the section (where it exists) and Arab numerals the chapter and the paragraph. For *The Wealth of Nations*, Roman numerals indicate the book and Arab numerals indicate the chapter (always), the part and the article (where they exist).

3 Adam Smith alternatively uses the expressions 'public good', 'interest of society' or 'public utility' in a largely interchangeable manner. In this text we have frequently employed the more contemporary terms 'general welfare', 'general interest' or 'general well-being'. It should be understood that for Adam Smith the general interest is always more than the sum of conscious individual interests. One should also note that the term 'utility' is developed in the first chapter of book IV of *The Theory of Moral Sentiments* as an aesthetic category that depends from the impartial spectator rather than as a quantifiable use-value that would correspond to its modern use.

4 Tribe distinguishes four major strands in Smithian studies: (1) the identification of modern economic concepts, (2) the establishment of the historical, cultural and political context, (3) interpretations of Smith as an early critic of market economics and (4) textual and linguistic analysis (Tribe 2002: 610). Our work extends to categories one and four. As far as textual analysis is concerned, it is important to approach the texts without preconceived notions and to *read* them patiently trying to identify the structure of their argument in their totality. Of course such a reading can benefit greatly from knowing the implications of a certain passage for modern economic theory or being aware of the historical and philosophical contingencies of the text.

2 Sympathy, communication, exchange – the horizontal world

1 Certain critics such as Young consider the sympathy mechanism radically opposed to the notion of self-interest, the principal motivating force in *The Wealth of Nations*. Such an interpretation, of course, loses the fundamental, even if partial, continuity between Smith's two major works.

2 The sympathy mechanism is neatly captured in David Hume's expression that 'the minds of men are mirrors to one another' (Hume 1739–40 (II.ii.5): 469). The citation stems from a chapter in the *Treatise* with the evocative title 'Of our Esteem for the Rich and Powerful', which shows the extent to which Smith benefitted from his older friend's work to develop the notion of the sympathy mechanism and the social function of wealth. In the same chapter Hume states:

> The *satisfaction* we take in the riches of others, and the *esteem* we have for the possessors may be ascrib'd to … sympathy, which makes u partake of the satisfaction of every one … Nothing has a greater tendency to give us an esteem for any person, than his power and riches; or a contempt, than his poverty and meanness: And … esteem and contempt are to be consider'd as species of love and hatred …
>
> Upon the whole, there remains nothing, which can give us an esteem for power and riches, and a contempt for meanness and poverty, except the principle of *sympathy,* by which we enter into the sentiments of the rich and poor, and partake of their pleasures and uneasiness.
>
> (ibid.)

See below our remarks on the 'social function of wealth' in *The Theory of Moral Sentiments*, which elaborates Hume's ideas.

3 This singular passage with its collection of instruments permitting to occupy oneself with one's body in an intimate manner (two of them regard the cleansing of bodily orifices), also motivates one more, as a counter-example, the importance of the sympathy mechanism and its overall positive assessment in Smith's work. The sympathy mechanism is ultimately the only reliable manner, by which the Smithian individual can hope to escape the prison, or 'island', of the antisocial physical passions that risk absorbing him.

4 The notion of 'design' that communicates a good's function and its role in marketing economic goods fits perfectly with Smith's view of the working of a market economy.

5 We disagree on this point with Jean-Pierre Dupuy who insists on the difference between the *homo oeconomicus* and the Smithian individual (Dupuy 1992: 89). This interpretation is the logical consequence of his denial of the social function of wealth.

6 One should note in the preceding quote the phrase 'the objects upon which his comfort and happiness in this life are *supposed* principally to depend'. Here as in other instances, Smith maintains the ambiguity between the normative point of view of the moral philosopher for whom 'fortune, rank and reputation' are not the true sources of happiness and the positive point

of view of the social scientist, for whom the objective drivers of behaviour are worthy subjects of study in their own right.

7 While it would be useful to undertake a systematic reformulation of Smith's representation of the working of the human mind with the help of modern psycholinguistic theory, this essay remains concerned with its implications for economic theory. Nevertheless, it is clear that the dichotomy 'signifier – signified' (*signifiant – signifié*) assumes a particular relevance here opposing the shared and socially accepted linguistic element with the individual, non-communicable chaos inside an individual's mind.

8 Dubœuf writes convincingly that in Adam Smith 'value, the nature of wealth that a good constitutes for men, can only be conceived through comparison, the display that constitutes it as wealth'(ibid.).

9 Françoise Dubœuf is correct in underlining the distinction between labour as a measure of value and labour as a source of value. However, we disagree with her when she states that this distinction implies a divergence between the cost of labour and the value of its output and hence a pre-Marxian criticism of the market economy by Adam Smith. Such an interpretation presupposes an objectivist view of distributional justice incompatible with the self-referential system of markets in Adam Smith. In the evolutionary perspective that Smith pursues, where ultimately only the propagation of society is recognised as an objective criterion, the reproduction of labour is its own reward and is already ensured by the notion of the subsistence wage. Paying a worker more than his subsistence wage is neither necessary nor desirable, since it would introduce potentially disturbing exogenous criteria into the otherwise smoothly proceeding mechanics of the economic system.

10 The Peircean tradition (according to the American semiotician Charles Sanders Peirce) in which Umberto Eco situates himself distinguishes three categories of signs: the symbols (for instance, a cross symbolising the Christian faith), the indexes (for instance, an arrow indicating a direction) and the icons (for instance, a photo that is 'like' its object).

11 'If we should enquire into the principle in the human mind on which this disposition of trucking is founded, it is clearly the natural inclination everyone has to persuade. The offering of a shilling, which to us appears to have so plain and simple a meaning, is in reality offering an argument to persuade one to do so and so as it is for his interest' (*Lectures on Jurisprudence A*, vi.56, quoted according to Dellemotte 2001: 6).

12 In his entry on "Competition" in *The New Palgrave*, George Stigler, cites the following passage from a popular encyclopaedia of the first half of the nineteenth century in England, the *Penny Cyclopedia* (1839):'It seems that the word monopoly was never used in English Law, except when there was a royal grant authorizing some one or more persons only to deal in or sell a certain commodity or article' (Stigler 1988: 532).

13 In a framework of comparative statics, the coexistence between a competitive industry and increasing returns demands strong and not very realistic assumptions such as effects internal to the industry and external to the firm as embodied in Marshall's 'representative firm'. Marshall's vacillations on this point were severely criticised by Sraffa and others (see, for instance, Sraffa1926). The critics, however, never sufficiently appreciated that the problems of the Marshallian approach stemmed from the overarching

ambition to remain faithful to Adam Smith's dynamic vision *and* to translate it into the modern language of static theory. To a large extent, Marshall's contradictions emerge in the process of formalising Adam Smith's original vision.

14 Hirschman is right to recall Helvetius in this context who writes in *De l'esprit*: 'As the physical universe is ruled by the laws of movement, so is the moral universe ruled by laws of interest (Hirschman 1997: 43). In the limits of the scientific knowledge of the 18th century, Newton's laws of movement permit in effect an exhaustive explanation of physical phenomena, since they determine with precision each position and every movement. A latter day disciple of Helvetius is Milton Friedman who in 'The Methodology of Positive Economics' (Friedman 1953) emphatically insists on the analogy between the structuring forces of gravity and self-interest (see Keppler 1998b).

15 Internal to economics, that is. Needless to say, the objective arbitrariness of much exchange value – and the necessarily perfect disinterest of economic science in exploring it – has provided ample ammunition to the numerous critics of economics throughout the past 250 years.

16 We make reference to the notion according to which Adam Smith added little or nothing to the contemporary stock of knowledge in economic theory as synthesised, among others, by Dugald Stewart, Francis Horner et Lord Lauderdale (see, for example, (Schumpeter 1954), (Rothbard 1995) or (Rashid 1998)). Despite the legitimate interest the question of priority and theoretical coherence may evoke in general, it is obvious that it entirely misses the essential point of Smith's contribution. This contribution is the development of the coherent vision of a world in which all barriers to competition and transaction costs for economic rationality to assert itself are progressively dismantled. This is due to the inexorable process of codifying all matters economic through the all-pervasive sympathy mechanism.

17 See J.H. Keppler (2007), "Smith – Debreu: Social Interaction and its Mathematical Metaphors: Origin and Conclusion of the Principal Scientific Research Project in Economic Theory" for a broader discussion of the structural parallels between the economics of Adam Smith and modern general equilibrium theory.

3 The vertical world of the impartial spectator

1 Dupuy, for instance, considers the impartial spectator a simple 'bystander' (Dupuy 1992: 91). On the basis of this (false) premise, the critic will inevitably identify 'contradictions' in Adam Smith's work, once the latter begins to develop his theory of the two tribunals (see below).

2 An interesting exception is Vivienne Brown's *Adam's Smith Discourse: Canonicity, Commerce and Conscience* (Brown 1994), which opposes the impartial spectator (he, who sees) to the invisible hand. Her analysis of the textual structure unfortunately does not develop these concepts beyond a general 'multiplication of the narrative voices' in *The Theory of Moral Sentiments.*

3 Once more, this passage confirms to which extent *The Wealth of Nations* is the direct but partial prolongation of *The Theory of Moral Sentiments.*

4 The hypothesis that Adam Smith qualified as a theist is supported indirectly by Hirschman, who associates him with religious thinkers such as Blaise Pascal or Giambattista Vico (Hirschman 1997 : 20). While determining the precise religiosity of Pascal or Vico would require a much broader discussion, they are both associated with relatively abstract and little personalised visions of God.

5 Smith attributes this hierarchy to the 'indigenous tribes of North America' and explains that in 'more opulent and civilised societies' age determines rank only amongst those who are equal in all other respects.

6 Edwin Cannan, the editor of the important 1904 edition of *The Wealth of Nations*, even maintains in his 'Introduction' that Adam Smith based his lectures at Glasgow university in the 1750s on Hutcheson's *System of Moral Philosophy* (Smith 1776: xlvii).

7 In a preceding chapter, Smith had argued that moral rules are formed according to a mechanism that is identical to the sympathy mechanism:

> It satisfies us that we view them [rules concerning what is fit and proper either to be done or to be avoided] in the proper light, when we see other people view them in the same light … Every body is eager to honour and reward them. They excite all these sentiments for which we have by nature the strongest desire; the love, the gratitude, the admiration of mankind … It is thus that the general rules of morality are formed.
>
> (Smith 1759 (III.4.7–8): 184–85)

8 'Before approaching the heart of the matter, I would like to show the blindness that results from the hypothesis of specialisation [the separation of the economic from other aspects of social life] for instance, in the case of Albert Hirschman (Dupuy 1988: 76, our translation).

9 Smith develops the opposition between ideal behaviour and sufficiently good behaviour, but considers here the notion of ideal behaviour as unrealistic, pedantic and characterised in certain instances by unjustifiable cruelty:

> The Stoical wise man endeavoured to enter into the views of the Great Superintendant of the universe, and to see things in the same light in which that divine Being beheld them … all those who had arrived at this state of perfection, were equally happy; so all those who fell in the smallest degree short of it, how nearly soever they might approach to it, were equally miserable. As the man, they said, who was but an inch below the surface of the water, could no more breathe than he who was an hundred yards below it … I cannot allow myself to believe that such men as Zeno or Cleanthes, could be the authors … of these stoical paradoxes … and am disposed to impute them rather to Chrysippus … who, from all that has been delivered down to us concerning him, seems to have been a mere dialectical pedant … .
>
> (Smith 1759 (VII.II.1.39–41): 341–42)

4 The paradoxical synthesis

1 See also Prévost who identifies the divergence between efficient causes and final causes at the origin of the invisible hand (Prévost 2002b).
2 The same link between wildly egotistical behaviour and the promotion of general welfare is also present in another passage of *The Wealth of Nations:* 'All for ourselves, and nothing for other people, seems, in every age of the world, to have been the vile maxim of the masters of mankind' (Smith 1759 (I.III.3): 437). This passage does not contain a reference to the invisible hand but limits itself to mention 'the silent and insensible operation of foreign commerce and manufactures' (ibid.).
3 The original citation reads:

> Das besondere Interesse der Leidenschaft ist also unzertrennlich von der Betätigung des Allgemeinen; denn es ist aus dem Besonderen und Bestimmten und aus dessen Negation, dass das Allgemeine resultiert. Es ist das Besondere, das sich aneinander abkämpft und wovon ein Teil zugrunde gerichtet wird. Nicht die allgemeine Idee ist es, welche sich in Gegensatz und Kampf, welche sich in Gefahr begibt; sie hält sich unangegriffen und unbeschädigt im Hintergrund. Das ist die *List der Vernunft* zu nennen, dass sie die *Leidenschaften* für sich wirken lässt, wobei das, durch was sie sich in Erscheinung setzt, einbüßt und Schaden leidet.
>
> (Hegel 1986: 49)

5 The ethics of morality: conclusion

1 Structurally, the double normative framework to which the Smithian individual is exposed between a vertical, ethical axis and a horizontal, moral axis resembles the double commandment of the Christ:

> The most important one [commandment] answered Jesus, 'is this: 'Hear, O Israel, the Lord our God, the Lord is one. Love the Lord your God with all your heart and with all your soul and with all your mind and with all your strength'. The second is this: 'Love your neighbour as yourself'. There is no commandment greater than these.
>
> (Gospel of Saint Mark 12: 29–31)

For Smith's world, the second commandment would need to be re-formulated 'Love yourself as your neighbour loves you'.
2 See also (Dermange 2003: 78 and 114) on this point.
3 Viner's case is characteristic for the contortions that, in particular, the most subtle and sincere critics have to undertake when trying to save a one-dimensional interpretation while accommodating Smith's complexity. Viner begins with noticing the multiplication of the 'names of the father' (see earlier) just to classify them in the following under the heading of a "well-meaning nature" whose ability to include manifestations of sympathy becomes its determining quality in *The Theory of Moral Sentiments.* In utter contrast, *The Wealth of Nations* is then considered to be based

entirely on self-interest. In the following, Viner dedicates his article to the enumeration of the exceptions to the principle of *laissez faire* that can be found according to him in *The Wealth of Nations.*

4 Edward Cannan remarks in a footnote that none of the possible sources of Smith (Seneca's *De ira* or the *Histoire romaine* of Dio Cassius) mentions the liberation of all the slaves (Smith 1776 (IV.7.2): 101), which thus seems to be a personal addition of the author.

Bibliography

Arrow, K. J. (1970) 'The Organization of Economic Activity: Issues Pertinent to the Choice of Market versus Non-Market Allocation', in Haveman, R. H. and Margolis, J. (eds) *Public Expenditure and Policy Analysis*, Chicago: Rand-McNally.

——(1979) 'The Division of Labour in the Economy, the Polity and the Society', in Driscoll Jr., G. P. (ed.) *Adam Smith and Modern Political Economy*, Ames, IO: Iowa State University Press.

Assoun, P-L. (2003) *Lacan*, Paris: Presses universitaires de France (PUF).

Bergson, H. (1932; 2000) *Les deux sources de la morale et de la religion*, Paris: Presses universitaires de France (PUF).

Brown, V. (1994) *Adam Smith's Discourse: Canonicity, Commerce and Conscience*, London: Routledge.

Campbell, R. H. and Skinner, A. H. (eds) (1981) *The Origins and Nature of the Scottish Enlightenment*, Edinburgh: John Donald.

Cannan, E. (1904; 1976) 'Editor's Introduction', in Smith, A. *An Inquiry into the Nature and Causes of The Wealth of Nations*, Chicago: University of Chicago Press.

Clark, J. M., Douglas, P. H., Hollander, Jacob H., Morrow, G.R., Palvi, M. and Viner, J. (1928; 1989) *Adam Smith, 1776–1926: Lectures to Commemorate the Sesquicentennial of the Publication of 'The Wealth of Nations'*, London: Kelley.

Coase, R. H. (1937) 'The Nature of the Firm', *Economica* 4: 386–405.

——(1988) 'Notes on the Problem of Social Cost', in *The Firm, the Market and the Law*, Chicago: University of Chicago Press.

Debreu, G. (1959) *Theory of Value: An Axiomatic Analysis of Economic Equilibrium*, New Haven: Yale University Press.

Dellemotte, J. (2001) 'Sympathie, échange et valeur: La sympathie à l'oeuvre dans The Wealth of Nations', paper presented at the IXe Colloque de l'Association Charles Gide, Strasburg, 27–29 September 2001.

Dermange, F. (2003) *Le Dieu du marché*, Genève: Labor et fides.

Diatkine, D. (1991) 'Présentation de *The Wealth of Nations*', in Smith, A. *Recherches sur la nature et les causes de la richesse des nations*, Paris: Flammarion.

Driscoll Jr., G. P. (1979) *Adam Smith and Modern Political Economy*, Ames, IO: Iowa State University Press.

Duboeuf, F. (2001) 'Travail commandé, travail incorporé, de Smith à Ricardo: analyse d'un malentendu', paper presented at the IXe Colloque de l'Association Charles Gide, Strasburg, 27–29 September 2001.

Dupuy, J-P. (1988) 'Au principe des approches communicationnelles du politique: la philosophie écossaise du XVIIIe siècle' *Hermès* 1 (*Théorie politique et communication*): 72–85.

——(1992) *Le sacrifice et l'envie: Le libéralisme aux prises avec la justice sociale*, Paris: Calmann-Lévy.

——(1993) 'A Reconsideration of *Das Adam Smith Problem*', *Stanford French Review* 17: 45–57.

Eco, U. (1984) *Trattato di semiotica generale*, Milano: Bompiani.

Edgeworth, F. Y. (1881) *Mathematical Psychics: An Essay on the Application of Mathematics to the Moral Sciences*, London: Kegan Paul.

Evensky, J. (2005) *Adam Smith's Moral System: A Historical and Contemporary Perspective on Markets, Law, Ethics, and Culture*, Cambridge University Press, Cambridge.

Foray, D. (2000) *L'économie de la connaissance*, Paris: La Découverte

Freud, S. (1974; 1997) 'Totem und Tabu', in *Fragen der Gesellschaft, Ursprünge der Religion,* Studienausgabe vol. IX, Frankfurt am Main: S. Fischer, 8th edition, pp. 287–444.

Friedman, M. (1953) 'The Methodology of Economics', in *The Methodology of Economics and Other Essays*, Chicago: University of Chicago Press.

Haakonssen, Knud (1981) 'What Might Properly Be Called Natural Jurisprudence?', in Campbell, R. H. and Skinner, A. H. (eds) (1981); reprinted in Haakonssen (1998).

——(ed.) (1998) *Adam Smith*, Dartmouth: Ashgate.

Hegel, G. W. F. (1986) *Vorlesungen über die Philosophie der Geschichte*, Collected Works vol. XII, Frankfurt: Suhrkamp.

Hirschman, A. O. (1977; 1997) *The Passions and the Interests: Political Arguments for Capitalism before Its Triumph*, 20th Anniversary Edition, Princeton, NJ: Princeton University Press.

Hollander, J. H. (1928a; 1989) 'The Dawn of a New Science' in Clark, J. M., Douglas, P. H., Hollander, Jacob H., Morrow, G. R., Palvi, M. and Viner, J. (1928; 1989) *Adam Smith, 1776–1926: Lectures to Commemorate the Sesquicentennial of the Publication of 'The Wealth of Nations'*, London: Kelley.

——(1928b; 1989) 'The Founder of a School', in Clark, J.M., Douglas, P.H., Hollander, Jacob H., Morrow, G. R., Palvi, M. and Viner, J. (1928; 1989) *Adam Smith, 1776–1926: Lectures to Commemorate the Sesquicentennial of the Publication of 'The Wealth of Nations'*, London: Kelley.

Hont, I. and Ignatieff M., (eds) (1985) *The Wealth and Virtue: The Shaping of Political Economy in the Scottish Enlightenment*, Cambridge: Cambridge University Press.

Hotelling, H. (1929) 'Stability in Competition', *Economic Journal* 39: 41–57.

Hume, D. (1739–40, 2000) *A Treatise of Human Nature*, Oxford: Oxford University Press.

Jakobson, R. (1987), 'Linguistics and Poetics', in Jakobson, R. *Language in Literature*, Cambridge, MA: Harvard University Press, pp. 62–94.

Keppler, J. H. (1998a) 'Externalities, Fixed Costs and Information', *Kyklos* 52: 547–63.

——(1998b) 'The Genesis of Positive Economics and the Rejection of Monopolistic Competition Theory: A Methodological Debate', *Cambridge Journal of Economics* 22: 261–76.

——(2007) 'Smith – Debreu: Social Interaction and its Mathematical Metaphors: Origin and Conclusion of the Principal Scientific Research Project in Economic Theory', paper presented at the International Conference, *General Equilibrium as Knowledge*, Paris, 6–8 September 2007.

Knight, F. H. (1921) *Risk, Uncertainty and Profit*, Boston: Houghton Mifflin.

Lacan, J. (1966a) 'Fonction et champ de la parole et du langage en psychanalyse', in Lacan, J. *Écrits*, Paris: Éditions du Seuil, pp. 237–322.

——(1966b), 'Le stade du miroir comme formateur de la fonction du Je telle qu'elle nous est révélée dans l'expérience psychanalytique', in Lacan, J. *Écrits*, Paris: Éditions du Seuil, p. 93–100.

——(1981) *Le Séminaire livre III: Les Psychoses*, Paris: Seuil.

Larrère, C. (1999) 'Les passions à l'age classique: intérêts et passions', paper presented at the CERPHI seminar 17 February 1999, http://cerphi.net/sem/larrere.htm. Date last accessed 25 February, 2010.

Marshall, A. (1890; 1920) *Principles of Economics*, 8th edn., London: Macmillan.

Mizuta, H. and Sugiyama C. (eds) (1993) *Adam Smith: International Perspectives*, New York: St. Martin's Press.

Muller, J. (1993) *Adam Smith in His Time and Ours*, New York: Free Press.

Pack, S. J. (1991), *Capitalism as a Moral System: Adam Smith's Critique of the Free Market Economy*, Aldershot: Edward Elgar Publishing.

Peil, J. (1999) *Adam Smith and Economic Science*, Cheltenham: Edward Elgar.

Pommier, G. (1996) 'Ethique et fin de l'analyse', in *Le dénouement d'une analyse*, Paris: Flammarion.

Prévost, B. (2002a) 'Adam Smith précurseur des philosophies de l'Histoire', *Revue de Philosophie Économique* 6: 57–81.

——(2002b), 'La métaphysique de la main invisible', *Kaïros* 20: 43–72.

Rae, J. (1895), *Life of Adam Smith*, London: Macmillan.

Raphael, D. D. (1975) 'The Impartial Spectator', in Skinner, A. S. and Wilson, T. (eds) *Essays on Adam Smith*, Oxford: Clarendon.

——(2007), The impartial spectator: Adam Smith's moral philosophy, Oxford: Oxford University Press.

Rashid, S. (1998) 'Adam Smith and the Cycle of Ignorance', in *The Myth of Adam Smith*, Cheltenham: Edward Elgar.

Ricardo, D. (1821; 2001), *On the Principles of Political Economy and Taxation*, Kitchener: Batoche Books.

Ricœur, P. (1990) *Soi-même comme un autre*, Paris: Seuil.

Rothbard, M. N. (1995) *Economic Thought Before Adam Smith: An Austrian Perspective on the History of Economic Thought*, Cheltenham: Edward Elgar

Rothschild, E. (2003) *Economic Sentiments: Adam Smith, Condorcet and the Enlightenment*, Cambridge, MA: MIT Press.

Schumpeter, J. A. (1954) *History of Economic Analysis*, New York: Oxford University Press.

Shakespeare, W. (1623; 1994) *Macbeth*, Muir, K. (ed.), London: Routledge.

Skinner, A. S. and Wilson, T. (eds) (1975), *Essays on Adam Smith*, Oxford: Clarendon.

Smith, A. (1759; 2002) *The Theory of Moral Sentiments*, Haakonssen, K. (ed.), Cambridge: Cambridge University Press.

——(1776; 1904; 1976) *An Inquiry into the Nature and Causes of The Wealth of Nations*, E. Cannan (ed.), Chicago: University of Chicago Press.

——(1980) *History of Astronomy*, in W. P. D. Wightman and J.C. Bryce, *Essays on Philosophical Subjects*, D. D. Raphael and A.S. Skinner, *The Glasgow Edition of the Works and Correspondence of Adam Smith*, vol. III, Oxford: Oxford University Press.

Sraffa, P. (1926) 'The Laws of Returns under Competitive Conditions', *Economic Journal* 36: 535–50.

Stigler, G. (1988) 'Competition', in Eatwell, J., Milgate, M. and Newman, P. (eds) *The New Palgrave: A Dictionary of Economics*, London: Macmillan.

Taylor, C. (1989) *Source of the Self: The Making of the Modern Identity*, Cambridge, MA: Harvard University Press.

Tirole, J. (1989) *The Theory of Industrial Organization*, Cambridge, MA: MIT University Press.

Tribe, K. (2002) 'Adam Smith, Critical Theorist?', *Journal of Economic Literature* 37: 609–32.

Viner, J. (1928; 1989) 'Adam Smith and *Laissez faire*' in Clark, J. M., Douglas, P. H., Hollander, Jacob H., Morrow, G. R., Palvi, M. and Viner, J. (1928; 1989) *Adam Smith, 1776–1926: Lectures to Commemorate the Sesquicentennial of the Publication of 'The Wealth of Nations'*, London: Kelley.

Waszek, N. (1984) 'Two Concepts of Morality: A Distinction of Adam Smith's Ethics and its Stoic Origin', *Journal of the History of Ideas* 45: 591–606; reprinted in Haakonssen, K. (1998), *Adam Smith*, Dartmouth: Ashgate.

Winch, D. (1978) *Adam Smith's Politics: An Essay in Historiographic Revision*, Cambridge: Cambridge University Press.

——(1993) 'Adam Smith: Scottish Moral Philosopher as Political Economist', in Mizuta, H. and Sugiyama, C. (eds) (1993) *Adam Smith: International Perspectives*, New York: St. Martin's Press.

Young, A. A. (1928) 'Increasing Returns and Economic Progress', *Economic Journal* 38: 527–42.

Young, J. (1997) *Economics as a Moral Science: The Political Economy of Adam Smith*, Cheltenham: Edward Elgar.

Index